THE

Quentin Blake

BOOK

THE
Quentin Blake
BOOK

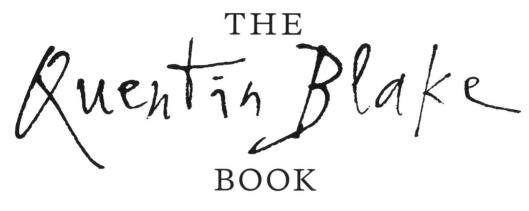

Jenny Uglow

WITH MORE THAN 300 ILLUSTRATIONS

T&H

Contents

INTRODUCTION Anything is Possible 7

CHAPTER 1 Youngest Contributor 11
Making a Start

CHAPTER 2 A Drink of Water 32
A Lifetime of Collaboration

CHAPTER 3 Dancing Frogs 60
From Patrick to Mr Filkins

CHAPTER 4 With Roald Dahl 88
The Odd Couple

CHAPTER 5   Don Quixote to Godot   110
             Classics and Unexpected Treasures

CHAPTER 6   Up the Wall   129
             Public Spaces and Hospitals

CHAPTER 7   Solo Sequences   149
             Personal Series: for exhibitions

CHAPTER 8   Twilight and Sunlight   167
             Personal Series: from book to gallery and back

CHAPTER 9   Worrying Times   197
             Some Feeling of Sympathy

CHAPTER 10   Imaginary Portraits   211
             Discovery through Drawing

CHAPTER 11   The Joy of Biro   225
             The Unexpected Line

             Author's Note   251
             Select Bibliography   252
             Index   254

All illustrations originally drawn in pen, ink and watercolour unless otherwise stated in the captions.

Anything is Possible

With a pencil anything is possible: cockatoos in the kitchen, a giant in sandals, an artist drawing in the air. For many years Quentin Blake's joyous, almost mobile creations have filled the imagination of children and adults across the world; his scratchy, leaping figures are the handwriting of a friend. Magic lies in the fluid line, the untidy wash of colour, the quizzical expression and odd gesture. The blank paper is a stage and every scene is full of action and feeling: exhilaration and delight, anger and alarm, sadness and grief. He can prick pomposity like a balloon, his work charged with sympathy for lonely souls and people battling against odds, fantastical and real.

This book celebrates Quentin's career, from teenage cartoons for *Punch* to his response to world suffering in the exhibition 'We Live in Worrying Times' in 2020, and the extraordinary drawings made during the pandemic. It follows his collaboration with authors, his re-imagining of classics like *Don Quixote* and *Candide*, and the invention of his own unforgettable characters, such as Mr Magnolia with his solitary boot, and Mrs Armitage on her bicycle.

A pioneer among the talented British illustrators of the late twentieth century, when new developments finally enabled good colour printing, Quentin became the first British Children's Laureate in 1999. Alert to the great tradition of illustration and its present wealth, and realizing there was no designated gallery, he led the drive to found the House of Illustration in 2014, which moved to a new home in Islington, north London, as the Quentin Blake Centre for Illustration, in 2022. Another cause for celebration.

Quentin with his work, 2007

Angel Pavement, 2004

 Distinctive though it is, Quentin's work can be unpredictable, even to the artist himself. He has always been open to different techniques, from pen, ink and watercolour washes to vast digital enlargements. He likes odd, ancient tools, a quill or a bamboo pen. 'You get a more adventurous feel from a scratch pen,' he says, remembering how a woman in France sent him a feather from a vulture's wing, that he sharpened into a quill: 'rather splendid'. He doesn't care if the watercolour escapes the lines: 'it makes it feel as if there is something happening.'

 There is always something happening in his work. It defies boundaries. It has leapt beyond the page to gallery walls, schoolrooms and hospitals, and knows no national borders. The many honours he has received haven't tempted him to slow down or rest on his laurels. At ninety he is full of visions and new ideas, hard at work amid shelves full of books, overflowing tables and plan chests. All he wants to do is to draw. He is, thank goodness, unstoppable.

An imagined view of the House of Illustration ahead of its move to New River Head, 2020.
Acrylic on watercolour paper

'This was painted on the spot during the BBC documentary
The Drawing of My Life using acrylic paint and brush on large
watercolour sheets.' QB

10

1

Youngest Contributor
Making a Start

As a child Quentin Blake was always drawing, finding a private script, a language of his own. Born in Sidcup, Kent, on 16 December 1932, he went to the local primary school and then, after a wartime evacuation to Devon, to Chislehurst and Sidcup Grammar School. His family were not artists: 'everything I learnt, I learnt at school,' he says. But he had plenty of time to draw, producing atmospheric sketches of the railway sidings behind his house and other buildings nearby. This was his setting, and he drew it with an eye alert for oddity and telling shapes – the high gantry, the old wheel, the tangle of wires.

A drawing of a schoolfriend revealed his sensitivity to mood, his evocation of a hidden interior life, while in scraperboard drawings for a story he wrote for the school magazine, the *Chronicle*, he showed that he could bring a pose to life: the boy deep in his book, or struggling into his heavy coat.

These finished studies were conventional enough, but his quick, informal sketches – like the rough drawing of an old house that seems to speak, or his view looking down at a Bermondsey Street corner – were more revealing, more personal, more indicative of what was to come.

Self-portrait of Quentin as a young boy, drawn for a retrospective exhibition in 2003. China marker on watercolour paper

Above, left: An early portrait of a schoolfriend, *c.* 1949.
Pencil on cartridge paper
Above, right: Scraperboard drawings for the school magazine, *c.* 1949

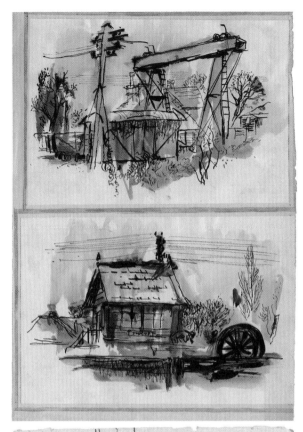

Above: Unidentified building, *c.* 1949.
Pencil on typing paper
Above, left: Railway sidings and signal box in Sidcup, *c.* 1949
Left: Post Office in Bermondsey Street, *c.* 1949
Pen and ink on cartridge paper

Quentin's own book, *Words and Pictures*, gives quick snapshots of key moments in these early years. These included a memorable school trip to London to see Marcel Carné's 1945 film *Les Enfants du Paradis*. Watching Jean-Louis Barrault as the clown, flopping like a puppet until he suddenly comes to life in mime, was a lasting lesson, a key to illustration as a way of 'telling the story by acting it'. Quentin took small parts himself in school plays, and perhaps this contributed to his sense of illustration as theatre: plot conveyed by action, gesture and expression, with minimum props, and the impact shown by the spectators' reactions (rabbits and mice are particularly handy and expressive, he says). An acute observer, Quentin can be a wicked mimic, and in his mind he 'acts' the people he is drawing, often making faces as he draws.

Another snapshot: Quentin at sixteen, waiting in the *Punch* offices off Fleet Street, 'full of heavy furniture and men in important-looking suits'. He had sent drawings to the magazine for a couple of years, and now he planned to tackle the editor himself. On his first visit he waited in vain (the secretary thought he must be the son of another visitor), but the second brought an offer of work and the editor congratulated him on being 'the youngest ever contributor'. He would draw for *Punch* for the next forty years. In one comic-strip page he put something of his own youthful delight in his work, showing a boy discovering the joy of modelling, utterly absorbed – thumping and squeezing and

'Children's Library', *Punch*, 1960s. Pen and ink on typing paper

moulding, ending simply with a mound of clay but with a beatific smile on his face.

It took time, though, to realize that he didn't need to sweat over a perfect drawing. In fact his roughs were livelier, more direct: once or twice the art director, 'though a man of very controlled and organized drawing himself', actually printed the rough in preference to the finished drawing. Quentin's impromptu-looking style had found a home.

Cartoon for *Punch* magazine, 1960s

Right: *Punch* cover,
1962. Pen, ink,
watercolour and chalk
on cartridge paper
Opposite: *Punch* cover,
1964. Pen, ink, wax
crayon and chalk on
Saunders board

The *Punch* commission meant a great deal. It linked Quentin to earlier artists, to George Cruikshank and John Tenniel, and the great Victorian illustrator Dicky Doyle, who started as a teenager and drew for *Punch* for many years. He could feel, too, that he was following his hero, Honoré Daumier, whose witty lithographs of daily life had appeared in *Le Charivari*, the French forerunner of *Punch*. (As a schoolboy Quentin bought a large hardback volume of Daumier lithographs for two guineas. The extravagance shocked his mother, but the book showed him that you can be a great artist, even in a newspaper.)

His own apprenticeship was like being 'an assistant in a blacksmith's shop or in a fifteenth-century artist's studio', starting with simple tasks and watching experienced craftsmen. He took note, for example, of Ronald Searle's eloquent, satirical drawing style, and the sophisticated, surreal cartoons of

' I made an intentional effort to vary my materials: pastels, oil pastels, watercolour pastels, coloured ink, wrapping paper – even the glass eyes supplied for the repair of teddy bears. What calls for more, if less evident, effort is to experiment with colour itself. I can draw without a sense of inhibition, but it took me time to get over a certain prejudice that the leaves of trees are green and that their trunks are brown and that the sky is blue, though to the eye they may be blue or purple or brown.' QB

the French artist André François, which made him see that a drawing could fill its commercial task but 'with panache: still be scratchy and instinctive, and badly behaved'.

In 1953, after his obligatory two years of national service in the army (during which he drew a booklet, *English Parade*, to teach soldiers who couldn't read), Quentin began reading English at Downing College, Cambridge, where F.R. Leavis held sway. Then, after a post-graduate certificate in Education at London University, he taught part-time at the Lycée Français in London. Ex-pupils remember him warmly, as an unconventional and inspiring teacher, but he soon decided that this was not for him. He would make a living by his art.

By the early 1960s work was coming in fast, offering a variety of opportunities. Covers for *Punch*, in particular, posed an enjoyable challenge in finding visual solutions that were always varied yet kept the essence of the magazine.

At the same time he began working for the *Spectator*. He explains: 'One of my Cambridge contemporaries was a friend of the editor of the *Spectator*, who commissioned him to do a number of covers. However, his style was

' As the features varied in subject and tone
I found myself producing something often
quite different from one week to the next.
It was rather like an actor getting experience
in a repertory company.' QB

Spectator covers
Opposite: Lolita, 1959; Christmas, 1960
Left: Summer books, 1963
Below: Children's Books, 1963; Soviet Writers, 1965
Overleaf: Autumn Books, 1965; Christmas, 1959

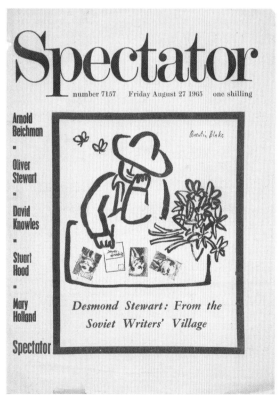

essentially decorative and so not very well able to cope with the variety of subjects. He was kind enough to get on to me. I began doing the covers and before long I found that I was doing more than anybody else.' Most of the covers could not be done until there was a decision about the main feature in the paper, 'consequently they were nearly all carried out within forty-eight hours, sometimes even less than that... For special numbers like the Christmas number, you know, I generally had more time.' He could cover the hot topics, like the publication of *Lolita*, and always managed to highlight key contents and writers. Authors' names nestle in the feathers of a Christmas bird or the spokes of a penny-farthing wheel.

SPECTATOR

Christmas Number

2'-

Hesketh Pearson

John Betjeman

Evelyn Waugh

Patrick Campbell

Cyril Ray

Roy Jenkins

Angus Wilson

Kingsley Amis

Bernard Levin

NUMBER 6856   FRIDAY, NOVEMBER 20, 1959

Cut paper designs for *Spectator* Arts pages, 1960s

Penguin covers for *Lucky Jim*, 1961, and *Eating People is Wrong*, 1962. Original drawings in pen and ink

For the *Spectator*, too, he drew some cut-paper headings for the arts pages, a pleasing foray into a different medium entirely.

By the early 1960s he was also designing covers for Penguin fiction. These included an untidy student with his floating pint, leaning against a field of red type, for Kingsley Amis's *Lucky Jim* in 1961 (on his website, Quentin notes that 'his eponymous hero has both feet on the unheroic ground of reality') and nervous-looking folk on plates for Malcom Bradbury's *Eating People is Wrong* the following year. They still look brilliant today.

A different side of Quentin Blake also found expression in these early years, a softer, romantic impulse that contrasts with his sharp comedy. He had done life-drawing at Cambridge, and prompted by the advice of the painter, illustrator and cartoonist Brian Robb, who taught at Chelsea School of Art, in the late 1950s he signed on at Chelsea, not to study illustration but as a part-time student in life-drawing. (In 1965, after Robb moved to the Royal College of Art, Quentin joined him as a part-time tutor in illustration, ultimately becoming Head of Illustration from 1978 until 1986.)

Above and opposite: Chelsea, life-drawings from memory, *c.* 1957

The sound anatomical understanding gained at Chelsea helped to give his leaping, bending, 'badly behaved' people their astonishing credibility. While he liked the life-drawing classes very much, he also developed his own individual approach: 'I found that to draw the model and then turn away and draw what you could remember (and then go home and draw it again in a different technique) was a practice I set myself.' He went a couple of times a week, for the best part of two years. 'I don't think I have ever been to a life class since,' he says, 'but that experience stays with me and I seem to be able to draw figures in any position from imagination.'

Girl in a Long Dress, c. 1970   *Nude Lady Pole-vaulter, c.* 1970. Etching

In his sketches, drawn in pen and ink with added crayon or watercolour, the nudes look away, preoccupied with objects on the table or a book on the floor. They are all the more interesting because they seem to hint at life outside, longing to be off. Eventually, in Quentin's work, they would be off and away – as in the lovely linear etching of one nude, pole-vaulting home with a laden shopping bag.

In the 1960s Quentin's drawings and paintings spiralled between delicate sketches, powerful nudes and fantastical images. All the time he was experimenting: drawing with a plastic quill, painting with house-painting brushes, trying heavy monotype print ink or wet pastel on typing paper. A friend suggested to Quentin that these somnolent nudes had a 'subaqueous' feel, a mood found in his later groups of swimmers. Drawings can free us from our

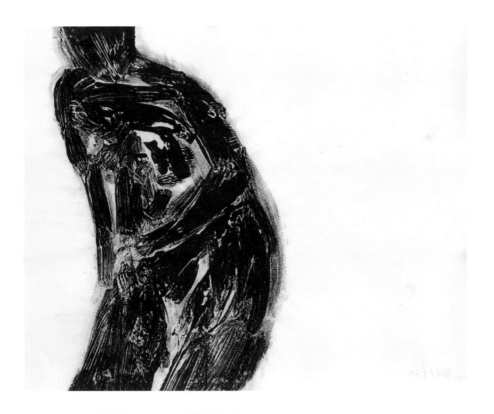

Top: *Hunched Figure*, 1960s. Monotype print on cartridge paper
Above: *Joker*, 1960s. Monotype print on cartridge paper

Above and opposite: *Faceless Nudes*, 1960s. Wet pastel on typing paper

'These were more emotional than naturalistic…
In some ways what they seem to be is the opposite
of my illustration – they're introspective, not very
active, the strokes are broad, not precise, etc.' QB

earth-bound state into other elements, diving into seas, flying in the air. Birds (often foreign to any ornithologist's description) are perpetual residents in his art. 'I have always liked drawing birds,' he says, 'I can't quite explain why, but it may be because like us, they are on two legs and have expressive gestures.' In his book *The Life of Birds*, 2005, he ponders on this, adding, 'I am not quite sure when they developed into a separate race of beings, parallel to ourselves and pursuing all our activities.' Certainly they took glorious form in 1971, when he illustrated an edition of Aristophanes' play *The Birds*. In this fanciful fifth-century BC satire on politics and utopias where the chorus, according to a stage direction, are 'stylized versions of different birds, each with a large beak mask' – two men arriving from Athens persuade them to build their own city in the sky, 'Cloud-Cuckoo Land'. The play was a gift to an imaginative artist, whose own work had already taken flight. And it gave him a different idea of 'acting' a story, flying across the white space of the page.

The Birds, 1971
Above, left: The Athenian, Pisthetaerus, with his surveyor's tools
Above, right: Bird talking to Heracles
Opposite: The goddess Iris flies in, escorted by the Hoopoe

' I found that I was treating the page as an open area where
the characters, in fancy dress, act out the story. I think
this approach – the page being the place where the story
happens – has been in the back of my mind ever since. ' QB

2

A Drink of Water

A Lifetime of Collaboration

The Wild Washerwomen, 1979

From the start of his career, Quentin had plenty to do, but by the late 1950s, he recalls, 'I had no idea how you arranged to get to illustrate a children's book. So I asked my friend John Yeoman to write one for me.' It was the start of a collaboration that would last for fifty years and more.

The first book that Yeoman wrote for Quentin to illustrate was *A Drink of Water*, published in 1960, full of people, birds and animals, including a monkey and a warthog. It was a gift for an artist who was good at conveying the quirky relations between humans and animals. The cover was a firework burst of deep-pink leaves, confident and full of zest.

Books with pictures are for fun and fantasy. They offer a realm of safety, as Jane Eyre finds, shutting herself behind the curtain with Bewick's *British Birds*: 'With Bewick on my knee, I was then happy.' Whatever age we are, as we read we learn, from something small, like the shape of a bird's wing, to something that affects our whole lives.

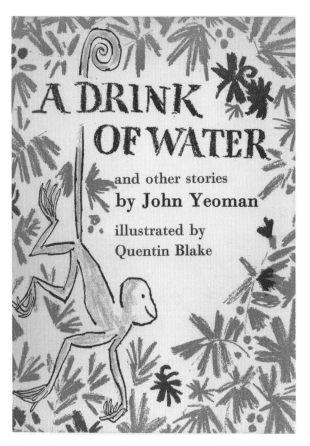

First-edition cover and interior artwork, *A Drink of Water*, 1960. Original drawings in pen, ink and wax crayon

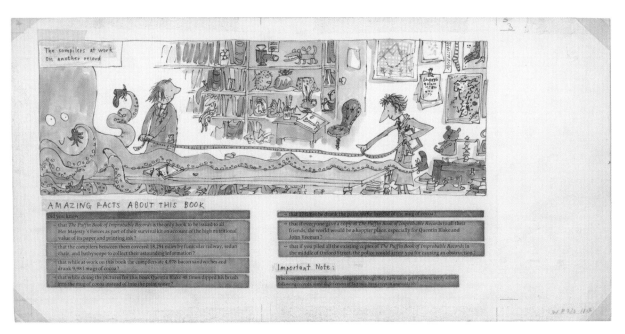

'The compilers at work on another record', Quentin Blake with John Yeoman in *The World's Laziest Duck and Other Amazing Records*, 1967

The most basic books are alphabets and counting books, and Quentin has done plenty of these, but he skips the didactic. Children learn almost by accident. In *Sixes and Sevens*, his design skills were evident in the way he arranged lively number groups around the pasted-in text – two mice, three schoolmistresses, six cockatoos and more – marching and sailing downstream across the page.

Three schoolmistresses, *Sixes and Sevens*, 1971

' The idea of the story is Barnaby picking things up in his raft
on the way to Limber Lee and how badly they all get on! ' QB

Yeoman and Blake also confronted the desire to learn the apparently impossible or, at least, never to be defeated. In *The Boy Who Sprouted Antlers*, Billy is impressed when the craft mistress, rattled by his inability to finish a wicker basket, declares: 'As long as you set your mind on something and try hard enough, there's nothing you can't do.' When his friends call this 'bilge' and suggest growing antlers, it's a challenge he can't refuse. The story is about a triumph of the imagination, and on the way, Billy has to take advice about natural history, anatomy - and even extinction.

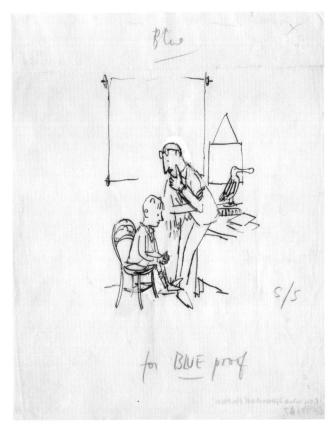 

The Boy Who Sprouted Antlers, 1961
Above, left: Billy with Mr Hanson, the vet. Pen and ink
Above, right: Colour overlay

Mouse Trouble, 1972

   Sometimes a problem demands an ingenious solution and a concerted effort. This is the case in *Mouse Trouble* when an angry miller faces a mouse invasion and buys a tabby cat. But the cat is too fat to catch anything and the mice become comically fond of it. When the miller decides to drown it, the mice set the cat free. The grateful cat lives happily in the attic, fed with the best titbits the mice can find, 'playing endless games of cat and mouse'.

The washerwomen take off, *The Wild Washerwomen*, 1979

Chaos erupts in *The Wild Washerwomen*, when seven overburdened women go on strike in the laundry, leaving the owner, Mr Balthazar Tight, with plenty of mud on his face. Freedom is intoxicating, and they certainly won't be tamed when seven woodcutters wade in to put them straight. Capitalism and sexism fall at the stroke of a pen.

One very popular book, this time allegedly down to earth, is *The Do-It-Yourself House that Jack Built*. Everyone who has wrestled with flat-pack furniture, let alone the building of a house, sees the joke, while for children this is a magical re-imagining of the old nursery rhyme, with the rhyme on one page and the near-disastrous efforts of Jack, opposite. In the end, of course, everyone will win.

Inevitably, some challenges seem impossible. In *The Hermit and the Bear*, the excited hermit (looking a bit like Quentin?) tries to give lessons to an eager talking bear, only to find every lesson sabotaged – but he finds, too, that it is worth it in the end.

This is the priest all shaven and shorn
   that married the man all tattered and torn
      that kissed the maiden all forlorn
         that milked the cow with the crumpled horn
           that tossed the dog
              that worried the cat
                that killed the rat
                  that ate the malt
                    that lay in the house
                    that Jack built.

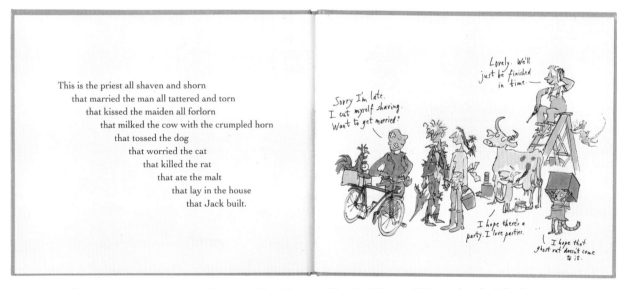

Artwork without captions (top) and final layout, *The Do-It-Yourself House that Jack Built*, 1994

The Hermit and the Bear, 1984. Pen and ink

Up with Birds!, 1998

Yeoman and Blake liked fantastical obstacles, even upside-down evolution. This is the problem facing the Fflyte family in *Up with Birds!* Birds have become pests – they don't fly, and they crowd on the ground. Hunting a solution, Mr Fflyte invents a flying machine using bicycles, balloons and feather-covered canvas: as the birds copy it, one by one they take off. Except the penguins.

In 1964, having sorted out his approach in his first books with John Yeoman, Quentin began working with Jonathan Cape, which would be his publisher for thirty years. Its list brought him many new authors. One of the first was J. P. Martin, whose *Uncle* books featured a rich, purple-clad elephant, his assorted cronies and his enemies from the decaying castle of Badfort, like Hitmouse or Jellytussle, with bristly, disgusting habits – great to draw.

Liz Williams, Quentin's archivist, explains that 'he drew the outlines then put glue on the sheets before adding detail – apparently the glue made the ink spread in interesting ways! It was, of course, clear when Quentin applied it.

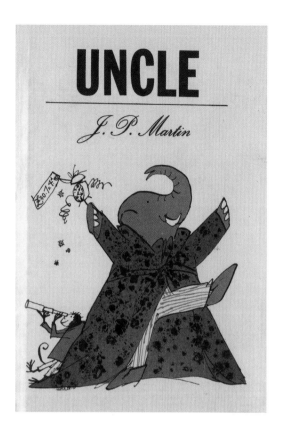

Left: First-edition cover for *Uncle*, 1964.
Pen and ink on Saunders board

Below, left: Uncle playing the cello, *Uncle*, 1964.
Pen, ink and glue on typing paper
Below, right: The Badfort crowd, *Uncle Cleans Up*, 1965.
Pen, ink and glue on typing paper

Opposite: Tom and Aunt Fidget Wonkham-Strong,
*How Tom Beat Captain Najork and His Hired
Sportsmen*, 1974

The intervening years and the presence of low levels of acid in the paper have turned the glue brown. A small curiosity!'

Quentin is adept at dreaming up details that bring out character. When he first read Russell Hoban's *How Tom Beat Captain Najork and His Hired Sportsmen*, the description of Aunt Fidget Wonkham-Strong in her iron hat gave him, he said, a 'very clear signal from the start; prompted by that I gave her eyes that gleam through her spectacles, and a trap-like mouth.' He also gave her a Victorian bustle and 'a floor-length dress that suggests that she may have no legs at all but some other form of locomotion'.

Aunt Fidget's attempts to stop Tom fooling around by hiring Captain Najork and his sportsmen seemed perfect to Quentin, 'so full of wonderful things to draw'. Of course, 'fooling around', the play of imagination, proves the key to success – and three more Captain Najork books followed.

Najork and the sportsmen arrive on their pedal-powered boat, *How Tom Beat Captain Najork and His Hired Sportsmen*, 1974

' *How Tom Beat Captain Najork* is, to my mind, a perfectly formed
moral fable about education. Consequently it was difficult for me
to imagine how it could have a sequel, but Russell does it expertly
by making it farce, and so a different order of being altogether.' **QB**

The Rain Door, 1986

Hoban's *The Rain Door* is less well known, but to Quentin it was 'as though Russell were inventing a myth'. In this powerfully evocative tale, the boy Harry follows the rag-and-bone man and his horse Lightning through the 'rain door' into a stony desert valley, to battle a ferocious, thunder-roaring lion – a mood that summoned lyrical watercolour drawings.

Each Hoban book was different. *Monsters*, Hoban's story of a boy who likes drawing monsters, posed a new problem. It was not enough, Quentin thought, to look over the boy's shoulder as he drew; instead, he had 'to learn once again how to do children's drawings'. Deliberately abandoning well-honed skills, he found his way back, realizing, as he did it, that he was even making the noises that children do while drawing. In the end, of course, the monsters take over.

Monsters, 1989

' Trying to do children's drawings was extremely difficult. An attempt
with my left hand didn't work, and I just had to eventually get used
to it, but there were a great many failures – if you can call them that.
What was additionally difficult was that they not only had to look
childish but also do special things which are mentioned in the story.
You will see that I also did them on squared paper to make them
look less like book illustrations.' **QB**

'John's monsters breathed smoke and fire', *Monsters*, 1989. Coloured fibre-tip pens on scrap paper

A decade later, in *Trouble on Thunder Mountain*, the O'Saurus dinosaur family set out to fight the building of a plastic mountain theme park, winning their way by joining with the moles and insects to create a real, rival mountain.

Their last book together, published in 2012, the year after Hoban's death, was very different. After seeing photos of Quentin's work in hospitals, Hoban sent him *Rosie's Magic Horse*. This tale, he says, which 'goes from the intimacy of the inside of a cigar-box to a flight by magic horse over cities and jungles, oceans and deserts', was irresistible. His drawings catch the tone: tender, idiosyncratic and packed with incident.

Trouble on Thunder Mountain, 1999

Rosie's Magic Horse, 2012

Cover artwork, *Because a Fire Was in My Head*, 2001. Chinagraph pencil and watercolour

Another collaboration has been with Michael Morpurgo, particularly on poetry to raise funds for Morpurgo's charity Farms for City Children. In Morpurgo's own collections and the anthologies *Because a Fire Was in My Head* and *Cock Crow*, Quentin's comedy makes the very soil, and the hard work, come alive.

A different, more naturalistic, style was needed for *Didn't We Have a Lovely Time!*, celebrating forty years of the charity. In the book Ito, a Vietnamese refugee, finds confidence in talking at night to the horse, and this time Quentin wanted to bring home the reality of the situation, showing 'that these are real adults, real children, so that one might almost feel that the drawings were made from life'.

Opposite: Cover artwork, *Muck and Magic*, 1995

Didn't We Have a Lovely Time!, 2016

On Angel Wings, 2006

And how to make the best-known stories feel fresh? Morpurgo's *On Angel Wings* tells of the nativity, remembered by the shepherd boy left behind to guard the flock. When the Angel Gabriel sweeps him up, the pages fill with colourful wings.

Quirky, resilient children fill Quentin's illustrations. When he read David Walliams's *The Boy in the Dress* in 2008, he says, 'I thought this was the real thing.' The book was funny, but what appealed most was 'the even-handed humanity of the book. It isn't about being gay or really even about transvestism. It's about a boy (who is also a gifted footballer) finding out about his own artistic tastes, and finding out about what it's like to be a girl.'

Next came Chloe hiding the smelly tramp in the garden shed in Walliams's *Mr Stink*. After this, however, Quentin says that he felt the author was steaming ahead so fast that he might not be able to keep up; much as he admired Walliams, he bowed out of illustrating more books in the series.

Sometimes we have to face things that are not merely challenging but unbearable. For years Quentin illustrated poetry and stories by Michael Rosen, beginning with the poems in *Mind Your Own Business* in 1974, in which Quentin's agile line drawings evoke the everyday atmosphere of children's lives, with rumbustious bursts of the fantastic.

The Boy in the Dress, 2008
Right: Lisa and 'Denise' talking to Raj.
Below: The football team in dresses.
Pen, ink and watercolour halftone

Mr Stink, 2009. Pen, ink and watercolour halftone

Mind Your Own Business, 1974. Pen and ink

Among the books they worked on was *Quick, Let's Get Out of Here*, which included poems about Rosen's small son Eddie: 'Eddie and the Gerbils', 'Eddie and the Nappy', 'Eddie and the Wallpaper'. But in 1999, at the age of eighteen, Eddie died suddenly of meningitis. The loss of a child is the worst horror to any parent. Professionals can help, but Rosen, notes Quentin, had first-hand experience and 'the skill and generosity to offer it to his readers'. Throughout *Michael Rosen's Sad Book* the terrible feelings of loss and darkness run side by side with evocative acts of memory. Worst of all for Rosen was the pretence of being happy while his soul was in despair – an image that Quentin re-drew many times before he felt it was right, and one that groups of the bereaved often use to understand and share.

The last words are: 'and candles. There must be candles.' As Quentin explains in his book *Beyond the Page*, it seemed right to end his flow of pictures with 'a final, wordless double-page spread of one candle, Rosen, and the photo of his son, so that the book ends in reflection and silence.'

Above and overleaf: *Michael Rosen's Sad Book*, 2004

31

3

Dancing Frogs

From Patrick to Mr Filkins

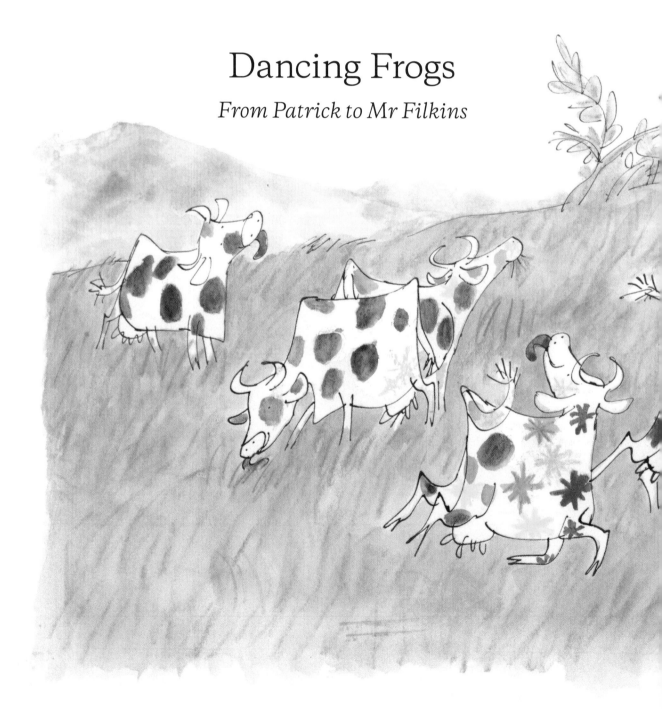

Preceding pages and above: *Patrick*, 1968. Pen, ink, coloured pencil and fibre-tip pen on Saunders paper

Quentin's early book illustrations were almost always in black and white, with two colours at most. Frustrated in getting a publisher to consider full colour, he finally succeeded by creating a story *about* colour. In *Patrick* – his first solo book, published in 1968 – a young man buys an old violin that makes things change colour when he plays it. More than this, it prompts sparks and feathers, turns cow's spots into multicoloured stars, and makes trees grow cakes, ice cream and hot buttered toast. After drawing the outlines in Indian ink, Quentin added watercolour, coloured ink and watercolour pastel – look closely and the colours seem to change before your eyes.

His excitement in colour was reflected almost forty years later in *Angel Pavement*. When the touring exhibition 'Magic Pencil', which he curated with Andrea Rose, arrived at the British Library in 2002, he found that the shop was selling pencils with one point, but made up of three colours, so that you can get a different one if you turn it. His angels, Loopy and Corky (who look like normal teenagers, apart from their magic-pencil wings), give these to the worn-down pavement artist Sid Bunkin, who can suddenly make drawings everywhere, even in the sky.

Angel Pavement, 2004. Pen, ink, magic pencil and watercolour

Jack and Nancy, 1969

Children's books welcome transformation: boundaries disappear, animals talk, children fly. In 1969, in *Jack and Nancy*, a wind-filled umbrella whisks the children to a tropical island, where they dive into lagoons and chat under palm trees, and finally, as in all good stories, come safely home.

Another form of magic lies in the skill of the circus. *Angelo*, in 1970, drew on the ancient *commedia dell' arte*, the origin of Pulcinella, ancestor of Punch. When Angelo dances on the tightrope, all the townsfolk turn out to cheer, in a riot of colour (see pages 2–3); but for the suspenseful night-time scene showing the rescue of Angelina, trapped in her uncle's house, Quentin tuned these down to subtle grey and gold. Art effects her escape.

Angelo, 1970. Pen, ink, crayon and watercolour

Quentin learned quickly how images themselves drive a story on. Indeed, for many children, the images *are* the story. A single central figure can grip the imagination, especially when combined with repetition and easy nonsense verse – a lesson Quentin claims to have gleaned from illustrating *Great Day for Up!* by Dr Seuss in 1974. This led to Mr Magnolia, who 'only had one boot', a word that allows great play with rhyme: a trumpet's 'toot-toot', fruit, scoot, hoot, the dinosaur 'brute'. In addition, almost invisibly, structure and onward drive come from an inlaid counting scheme: the five fat owls who perch on Mr Magnolia's bed, the ten spikes sticking up on the dinosaur's back.

Opposite and above:
Mister Magnolia, 1980

The furthest that Quentin took storytelling through images was in *Clown*, in 1995. The book has no words yet the story is full of drama, from the commotion of Clown dashing through the streets or being hurled from a high window, to the quiet, sympathetic looks at urban life. A woman, holding her nose in disgust, throws Clown and other old toys into a bin, but he escapes, wearing a pair of large stripy trainers from the dustbin, that give him the power to run fast. Setting out to save his fellow toys, on the way he rescues a young girl coping with her baby brother while her mother works. At the end the run-down flat provides a transformation scene as good as a pantomime, and Clown, his work done, turns back into a floppy toy again.

Clown, 1995
Above: Talking to a toddler, and being placed in a group photo
Opposite: cover artwork

Top: Mrs Armitage choosing a horn, *Mrs Armitage on Wheels*, 1987
Above: Meeting Uncle Cosmo and the bikers, *Mrs Armitage, Queen of the Road*, 2003

Quentin's stories often feature people who find their own way of dealing with difficult or strange situations, like Mr Magnolia, or who meet adventure in unexpected places, like Mrs Armitage joyfully crashing and honking her way on her bike, with her dog Breakspear.

Other stories, too, show people finding ways to deal with life on their own. *The Green Ship*, the most poetic of Quentin's children's books, conjures a summer long past, when the narrator and his sister discovered a group of trees in a nearby garden that looked just like a green ship, with masts and tall lookouts. Their neighbour Mrs Tredegar had married a ship's captain, who was lost at sea: in this arboreal ship, she takes the children on an imagined voyage, across seas and through a terrible storm. The summer passes, and year by year the untrimmed trees get back their old shape; soon there will be no way of knowing that they were once a green ship, but the story remains, a tribute to childhood, friendship and summers past.

The Green Ship, 1998

The Green Ship, 1998

The Story of the Dancing Frog is another story within a story, told by a mother to her child. It could, as Quentin has said, be told without the pictures – but what a loss that would be. The telling is shown in small sepia drawings of great tenderness, while the story told is full of colour. A young widow, Gertrude, tours the world with her new friend, George, the dancing frog, seen in fabulous poses with stars like Mistinguett and Fred Astaire – adult jokes that never trouble a child's enjoyment.

The Story of the Dancing Frog, 1984

Simpkin, 1993

' Simpkin acts his life. He is such a nuisance simply because,
like most children, he is in the ecstasy of being.' **QB**

Dancing is only one kind of movement in these mobile and anarchic books, and their fizzing energy is encapsulated in Quentin's creation of Simpkin, who rushes up and down and round and round, causing chaos at every turn.

Even housework can become a joyful dance, as we see in *All Join In*. Who cares if there is even more mess afterwards? The pleasure is in doing things, rather wildly, together.

Domestic life has its demands, not least the arrival of a new being. After Quentin worked on designs for maternity wards (see pages 146-7), he compressed the alarms and hopes of parenthood into *Zagazoo*, where the astonished George and Bella are confronted by a baby, unwrapped from a dazzling coloured

All Join In, 1990

Zagazoo, 1998

parcel. The gift, however, becomes in turn a squawking vulture demanding food (baby), a messy warthog (first self-feeding), a clumsy elephant (toddler), a dragon (alarmingly destructive small child) and eventually a disturbing, hairy monster, the baffling – and baffled – teenager. Children love the transformations, and parents laugh in recognition.

The impulse to care for another, however difficult, and the need to finally let them go, are touchingly conveyed in *Loveykins*, where Angela Bowling finds a baby bird, blown out of his nest, and takes him in. 'Augustus' is the child she never had, but under her fostering he grows into a rather demanding and terrifying bird. Eventually he flies the nest, but a bond endures; every now and then he drops in with the gift of a dead mouse or a few beetles, and in freedom his wings spread wide.

Loveykins, 2002

The Life of Birds, 2005
Top: Adolescence
Above: Up Against It. Watercolour pencil

Above and overleaf: *Cockatoos*, 1992

It's not surprising that this independent darling is a bird, a favourite theme. Eventually, birds and people would merge in a book of their own – *The Life of Birds* – at once recognizably avian and human, a flock of individual beings.

The cheekiest birds of all are the gang in *Cockatoos*, who hide everywhere they can find in an old house, to the despair of their owner, who fears he has lost his feathered friends – a beautiful hide-and-seek book.

Unusually, these pictures have detailed settings and a wealth of props, making finding the cockatoos a greater game. The house was based on one Quentin saw in France – he eventually bought a house himself in Charente-Maritime – and one can feel his love of the country, from its fragrant cookery to its stalls piled with brocante, in the junk that fills this attic.

France has played an important part in Quentin's life. He has been published there since the 1980s, has curated exhibitions and worked with hospitals and schools, and he was honoured as an Officier des Arts et des Lettres in 2007 and a Chevalier de la Légion d'Honneur in 2014. As his friend and publisher Christine Baker, director of Gallimard Jeunesse, says, he is hugely popular in France: 'He has a very witty sense of observation, which goes with the French sense of irony and sarcasm, but always with this kindness, and this generosity, and benevolence.' In 2000, collaborating with the teachers of Charente-Maritime and 1,800 French-speaking children from across the globe, he created *Un bateau dans le ciel*. The theme was *'l'humanisme'* – shown unaffectedly in the way that the children on their magical round-the-world flight help people they meet, who face prejudice, war and the many hardships of life.

Self-portrait as a frog, to demonstrate his links with France, *c.* 2000

Un bateau dans le ciel, 2000. Translated as *A Sailing Boat in the Sky*, 2003

All Quentin's solo books have a low-key optimism, a belief in tolerance and in the ability of people to help each other. That optimism is still there in recent books like *The Weed*, inspired by seeing a small weed flowering next to some pavement railings. In *The Weed* – a plea for the environment in a future that is 'hard, dry and difficult' – the Meadowsweet family climb up from a deep crack in the earth, with the help of their mynah bird, Octavia, and a magical seed. The green power of nature will, perhaps, conquer in the end.

Opposite and above: *The Weed*, 2020

Mr Filkins in the Desert, published in 2021, describes another kind of triumph. Setting off to see his family on his ninetieth birthday, Mr Filkins crosses the desert with his parasol, picnic and vital sparkling mineral water, ducking dangers and meeting strange creatures like the forty-legged Grindgle, and is saved from disaster by his compassion for the prone purple beast.

Time and age, Quentin Blake tells us all, need not put a damper on hope or kindness. Mr Filkins gets there in the end, 'and what a birthday party it was!'

Cover (above) and interior artwork, *Mr Filkins in the Desert*, 2021

4

With Roald Dahl

The Odd Couple

For many readers the names of Roald Dahl and Quentin Blake are inseparable. In over twenty books, Quentin's line drawings brought Dahl's creations to life in all their preposterous, diabolical oddity. There was a powerful creative chemistry between author and illustrator and they worked together for forty years, beginning in 1978, when Dahl's publisher Tom Maschler at Jonathan Cape (which had published *Uncle* and *Patrick*) asked Quentin to do sample drawings for *The Enormous Crocodile*. To make the pantomimic beast at once fantastic and dangerous, he thought of the crocodile in Punch and Judy shows, giving his croc a great set of saw-like teeth – 'teeth for eating children with' – although they pose no problem for Trunky the elephant, who sends him whirling into space.

The Enormous Crocodile demanded bright, almost luminous colours. By contrast, the next book, *The Twits*, a darker, brutal story, asked for black and white for its prison-like world, and a hard nib to give the mood (and to show Mr Twit's beard, 'which had to look like a lavatory brush'). The expressions

Preceding pages: Hampshire House, *The Giraffe and the Pelly and Me*, 1985
Above: *The Enormous Crocodile*, 1978

The Twits, 1980. Pen and ink on watercolour paper

speak volumes, as the couple play their cruel practical jokes – witness Mrs Twit's alarm as she is stretched beneath gas-filled balloons, and Mr Twit's glee as he prepares to tie another one.

George's Marvellous Medicine followed a year later, with eight-year-old George Kranky hunting for ingredients (all fatally toxic) for his wild concoctions. In George, Quentin shows the dangerous unpredictability of fantasy but also its powerful allure: 'For a few brief moments he had touched with his finger-tips the edge of a magic world.'

Over the years Blake and Dahl worked out a way of approaching each book. First Quentin produced rough sketches of possible scenes and incidents, and more detailed ones of his first vision of the characters, following descriptions in the text. Then he took these down to Dahl's home at Great Missenden. His feelings on first meeting Dahl – 'a very tall man who put dreams into children's heads', as Quentin described him to Nicolette Jones in a *Sunday Times* interview

George's Marvellous Medicine, 1981. Pen and ink on watercolour paper

in 2016 – and on seeing him with his granddaughter Sophie, would be reflected in the giant's tender relationship with the character Sophie in *The BFG*.

When *The BFG* was first set at the printers, with the drawings in black and white, Quentin received an alarming phone call: 'He's not happy.' Dahl was unhappy, not with the illustrations, but because there weren't enough of them. So they started all over again, with Dahl writing a list of scenes he would like to see. Then they went through them, adjusting drawings – and sometimes text – until they seemed right. Quentin changed his style from the thin-nib version that gave the BFG 'a rather clown-like face', to a more realistic approach that would let him convey nuances of mood and emotion.

Opposite: An early version of the BFG eating at the palace, 1981. Pen and ink on watercolour paper

The BFG as he eventually appeared in 1982

' I can remember he did say, when people talked about the BFG,
"They see what Quent draws," which was very nice of him.' QB

Still, a problem remained. In the original text the giant wore a long leather apron, but the illustrations showed that this would clearly make jumping or running difficult. In the television programme *Quentin Blake: The Drawing of My Life* in 2021, Dahl's widow, Felicity ('Liccy' to Quentin), remembered: 'There were many, many sketches of the BFG – with an apron, without an apron, and then "that wasn't right – what about a waistcoat?"... all done over very jolly dinners on our big dining room table. To watch Quentin with a pad of paper, and Roald talking about the book and the characters in it – the pencil contained magic... Really Roald and Quentin were like a pair of comedians. They were an "Odd Couple".'

The leather apron vanished but the problem of the BFG's footwear remained. Dahl damned his knee-length boots as 'dull'. Ideas were tried without success, until one day Quentin received a parcel in the post, containing a large, strange sandal; it was Norwegian and one of Dahl's own. The BFG wore them straight away.

Matilda, published six years after *The BFG*, posed another sartorial problem. Dahl's first description of the terrifying Miss Trunchbull's clothing was so

Matilda, 1988

extreme that illustrations following it faithfully made her look 'like a fascist general'. Gradually they modified her outfits until she looked feminine but alarming, someone 'who could have been an Olympic athlete'. To sharpen the contrast, Quentin felt he had to make Matilda very small, but she also had to be outstandingly intelligent, so to show this he gave her the face of an older child, but a touching one - shown in her rapt expression as she reads, and in her upward glance at the looming Miss Trunchbull.

If Quentin could manage crocodiles and headmistresses and bearded Twits, he could also convey the real evil and violence, the grimmer sides of Dahl's stories. There's often a playful touch of humour, but the monstrous characters, like the evil witches and the horrific aunts in *James and the Giant Peach*, are still satisfyingly scary. Thus the Grand High Witch in *The Witches*, who 'reckons on doing away with one child a week', can appear as a seductive handbag-waving woman, but when she strips off her mask, she looks like a classical Fury. Yet the hags are no match for the boy's Norwegian grandmother cosily smoking in her chair. Together they rescue Bruno, who has been turned into a mouse. As the grandmother says, with a hug, 'It doesn't matter who you are, or what you look like, as long as somebody loves you.'

The Witches, 1983
Opposite, left: The Grand High Witch with Bruno Jenkins
Opposite, right: The Grand High Witch unmasked
Above: Grandmama talking to the mouse-boy
Pen, ink and chinagraph pencil

When he tackled *Roald Dahl's Revolting Rhymes*, a tough and transgressive retelling of fairy tales, Quentin avoided putting too many horrors on the page, preferring to suggest rather than show (except in *Cinderella*, where the ugly sister's head comes off with a sweep of the sword, 'like a door-knob that might be fitted on later'). But suggestion can be even more frightening. We shiver at the sight of the wolf licking his lips with his long red tongue, as he drools over the grandmother's spectacles and knitting on the floor.

In *The Giraffe and the Pelly and Me*, the adventure of Billy and the Ladderless Window-Cleaning Company, the only threat is a luckless cat burglar. The whole fantasy of ladders let Quentin play with perspective, in great horizontals, like the 677 windows of Hampshire House, and in comic verticals like the giraffe's absurdly extendable neck – a superb use of space on the blank vertical page. Throughout, he could also enjoy the pelican with its flexible beak and the singing and dancing monkey, the 'me' of the title song.

Jack selling his cow for beans, *Roald Dahl's Revolting Rhymes*, 1982.
Toner and watercolour

The Wolf putting on Grandma's clothes, *Roald Dahl's Revolting Rhymes*, 1982.
Toner and watercolour

Quentin Blake and Roald Dahl discussing *The Giraffe and the Pelly and Me, The Roald Dahl Treasury*, 1997

' Roald was a very different person from me, and in a way that
was good, because if you're a double act you don't want to be
two versions of the same person – there's that contrast, a slight
tension almost.' **QB**

Architecture and windows, as a stage set, posed an engaging puzzle a few years later, when he came to illustrate *Esio Trot*. The action takes place in two flats, one above the other: the shy Mr Hoppy lives above, with his plants, secretly in love with Mrs Silver, who lives in the flat below with her tortoise Alfie. To get round the restricted setting, Quentin behaved like a filmmaker: 'Every camera angle has to be used,' he says. He drew horizontal long-shots, verticals to show the action against the city skyline, close-ups to reveal the happiness of Mr Hoppy, winning his love by an elaborate tortoise trick. In the layout, too, his role as designer came into play, something he greatly enjoys, making word and image work together.

Esio Trot was the last of the books published before Dahl's death. In the decade that followed, Quentin would illustrate many of Dahl's early books, published before their collaboration began. These included enduring classics such as *James and the Giant Peach* (Dahl's first children's book, from 1961) and *Charlie and the Chocolate Factory* (from 1964), and the distinctive drawings gave them a new life.

Esio Trot, 1990
Above, left: Mr Hoppy and Mrs Silver on their balconies
Above, right: The tortoise outgrows his house

James and the Giant Peach, 1995

Charlie and the Chocolate Factory, 1995

Other newly illustrated Dahl classics in the 1990s include *Danny the Champion of the World*, from 1975, and the clever, mischievous *Fantastic Mr Fox*, which first appeared in 1970.

The books stayed in print, read by a new generation of children, who saw them through Quentin Blake's eyes. Some years later, a different task faced him. In 2015, a year before the centenary of Dahl's birth, and the thirtieth anniversary of *The BFG*, which prompted many celebrations, the Dahl Estate asked if he could illustrate *The Minpins* to fit the standard Penguin format. The original version of 1991 would stay in print, with Patrick Benson's illustrations, but its format wouldn't work as a paperback, so, to avoid confusion, the new version, with Quentin's drawings starring a rebellious Billy with sticking-out hair, was re-titled *Billy and the Minpins* for its publication in 2017.

In two rather different books, Quentin came even closer to Dahl. One was the reissue of *Boy: Tales of Childhood*, originally published in 1984. This was 'not an autobiography', said Dahl, but a book drawing on some things that happened, 'that I have never forgotten'.

Danny the Champion of the World, 1994

Fantastic Mr Fox, 1996

Above: *Billy and the Minpins*, 2017

Opposite, clockwise from top left: A mouse in a jar of sweets,
the headmaster's cane and smelly pipe, Roald Dahl in his
Repton uniform, *Boy*, 2012.
Pen, ink and chinagraph pencil on watercolour paper

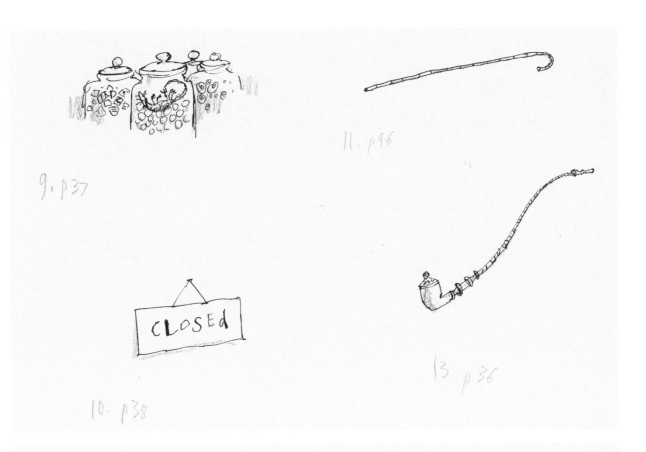

9. p37

11. p96

CLOSEd

13 p36

10. p38

Quentin illustrated *Boy* for the Dahl Estate in 2012, following it with an expanded version for Dahl's centenary four years later. His drawings perfectly convey the grotesquerie and mischievous innocence of Dahl's early years. But twenty years before, he had already accompanied a much older Dahl, in the watercolours for *My Year*, based on a diary kept by Dahl in the last year of his life (he wrote an essay a month, specially for Puffin books). *My Year* mixed an idiosyncratic account of the passing months with childhood reminiscences and advice on such things as winning at conkers and getting rid of moles. To evoke this, Quentin painted bees, frogs, mushrooms and eager fledglings opening their beaks for worms, but he also conjured up the personal experience of the changing seasons, from the promise of bulbs in spring and a cool room in the heat of summer to the crackle of November fireworks. Every scene follows Dahl's own injunction – which could also be Quentin's own – to 'look at the world with glittering eyes' and to find magic in unexpected places.

March, *My Year*, 1993

August, *My Year*, 1993

November, *My Year*, 1993

5

Don Quixote to Godot

Classics and Unexpected Treasures

The Folio Society produces beautiful editions of classic books, with carefully chosen endpapers, fine bindings and gold tooling. They have rather a serious air. So it's good when you take one out of its elegant slipcase and encounter Quentin Blake, irreverently alive.

Quentin is a voracious reader, in both English and French. His work for the Folio Society began with illustrations for Lewis Carroll's *The Hunting of the Snark* in 1976, followed by modern novels including Stella Gibbons's *Cold Comfort Farm*, Evelyn Waugh's *Scoop* and *Black Mischief*, and George Orwell's *Animal Farm*. In *Pens, Ink & Places* he writes of his long collaboration with the Folio Society editor Joe Whitlock Blundell, 'with him arriving by bicycle at my studio, or at the French Institute, or at some other (as he might say) congenial rendezvous'.

One of Quentin's talents is spotting the moment when an illustration can both carry the story and cast it in a different light. In Cervantes's *Don Quixote*, which he illustrated in 1995 and again to mark the book's quatercentenary ten years later, he homed in on key scenes like Quixote tilting at windmills or

Preceding pages: *Riddley Walker*, 2017
Above: Quentin thinking of Don Quixote for the cover of the *Royal Society of Literature Review*, 2015

Frontispiece (left) and Don Quixote looking down at Sancho Panza, *Don Quixote*, 1995

Sancho Panza being tossed in a blanket, but many drawings here are quieter in mood, looking forward to the lonely travellers of his future drawings, driven by dreams.

Next, for Victor Hugo's *The Hunchback of Notre Dame*, Quentin effortlessly conjured the mood of this great Gothic novel in blue halftones, with the moonlit cathedral standing squat against a stormy sky, while his portrayal of Quasimodo, the half-blind, deaf young hunchback, riding the great bell to make it ring, is more delicate, intensely physical and touchingly sympathetic.

Quentin also made his own suggestions. The first of these, in 1991, was an old favourite, Cyrano de Bergerac's *Voyages to the Moon and the Sun*, bought from a bookstall along the Paris quays. He had started to illustrate it simply

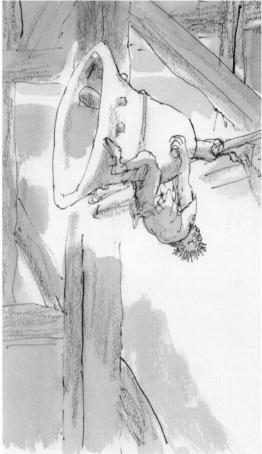

The Hunchback of Notre Dame, 1998
Above: The Cathedral by moonlight
Right: Quasimodo riding a bell

for his own pleasure, and one can see the fascination. First published in 1657, the *Voyages* have been described as the 'first science fiction classic', a precursor of *Gulliver's Travels*, with stories full of invented worlds, discussions of manners, religion, sex and bizarre scientific ideas and gadgets, like a musket that brings down birds ready-stuffed for the oven. Twenty years later he produced another, larger version, with twenty new drawings, giving them full elbow room on the page.

' In these invented worlds there are people much larger than we are, so there are differences of scale. They wear no clothes, so there are opportunities for life-drawing. There are aristocrats who communicate by playing the lute and working people who communicate by gesticulation. Indeed, the possibilities of all kinds of activity are manifold.' **QB**

Voyages to the Moon and the Sun, 1991
Left: Cyrano naked on a balcony
Above: Cover of the 2018 edition

Cyrano firing a blunderbuss, *Voyages to the Moon and the Sun*, 1991

Picaresque works, like Quixote's encounters in Spain or Cyrano's adventures in space, offer intricate, complicated shifts of mood, stories within stories, fantastic coincidences and reversals of fortunes. But they also share an underlying theme that recurs in Quentin's own books and in his later drawings: the hunt for nuggets of good or flashes of magic in a grim, inhospitable world. When he illustrated Voltaire's satirical novella *Candide, ou l'Optimisme*, he evoked the elegance of eighteenth-century France but also its complacent pomposity, embodied in Dr Pangloss's dictum that 'all is for the best, in the best of all possible worlds.' Far from it. Step by step, in story after story, Voltaire's young hero finds prejudice, corruption, political and religious intransigence, and violence. In inset line drawings and full-colour plates, Quentin echoed Voltaire's dark mix of farce, dismay and understanding, showing a talent for tragedy as well as comedy. Published in 2011, using Tobias Smollett's 1762 translation and introduced by Julian Barnes, the limited edition proved so popular that it was reissued with the same illustrations five years later.

Candide, 2011
Above, left: The hanging of Dr Pangloss
Above, right: The King of El Dorado

With Senator Pococurante in his library, *Candide*, 2011

Quentin took a different approach in 2013 with *Fifty Fables of La Fontaine*, deciding not to pursue the narrative and look for effective scenes, but to trust in the author. 'In almost every fable,' he says, 'La Fontaine actually "gives you the moment"; what you have to do is try to get it right.' Although the fables are chiefly known in children's versions, he points out that they were not written for children at all. They are not all about animals, but more about the weaknesses and idiosyncrasies of people, treated in a leisurely and relaxed way. He was glad to illustrate an edition for adults; indeed, he enjoyed it so much that he often drew a perfectly good illustration again, just 'to see if I could get a further nuance out of it'.

' The fables must have been a relaxed form of entertainment,
 with an air of – it's hard to find a suitable word that isn't
 French: *insouciance, désinvolture*. They were both innocent
 and knowing.' **QB**

'The Cricket and the Ant' and 'The Lion brought down by Man', *Fifty Fables of La Fontaine*, 2013

Quentin's next suggestion, Apuleius' *The Golden Ass*, also contained a
whole box of inset stories and folk tales. Eager to learn about magic, the hero,
Lucius, tries to turn himself into a bird but is transformed by mistake into
an ass – doomed to blunder ludicrously on, through many adventures, until
the goddess Isis takes pity on him and returns him to human form. The only
surviving Greco-Roman novel, from the second century AD, *The Golden Ass*
is in many ways an early version of the picaresque, enchanting in all senses.
Quentin also liked the contrast between the lyrical, fairy-tale romance of
Psyche 'and the very down-to-earth accounts of physical activities'.

The Golden Ass, 2015
Above, left: The witches Panthia and Meroe with torches
Above, right: Lucius the ass with a naked woman

From a story two thousand years old, he moved to a dystopic vision set two thousand years in the future. In Russell Hoban's *Riddley Walker*, a Kentish boy writes his 'autobiography' after a nuclear disaster has plunged his world into a second Iron Age. Here another wandering narrator speaks his own life in a distinctive, eccentric dialect, and Quentin had to find a style to reflect this. He had been illustrating Hoban's children's books since 1974, and in 1980 Hoban had written a dedication in Quentin's copy of *Riddley Walker*, using Riddley's voice and spelling. In Quentin's note in the Folio edition, he used the first line, '*Draw* is a Intersting word', as his title.

For this book, Quentin made the shapes large and awkward, sprawling outside the text or page, and drew with different quills, saying that the idea of contemporary printing reproducing marks made by ancient tools had great appeal: 'you feel you are taking part in the history of the craft – but more important is the character of the marks they make. They can be coarse, as appropriate to the situations of Riddley's narrative language, but also quite precise in detail of gesture and expression.'

Russell Hoban's dedication in Quentin's copy of *Riddley Walker*, 1980

Cover artwork, *Riddley Walker*, 2017

The heads of Granser and Goodparley on poles, *Riddley Walker*, 2017

' In some ways I am reluctant to talk about the illustrations… their
effect on the spectator, however arrived at, is their success or
failure. But the process is of great interest to me, and not least
here, where the invitation was to create images which on the one
hand were my drawings and on the other would be near Riddley's
primitive text. Incident – activity – is fascinating to me, but what
seemed to me here was the atmosphere – the darkness, the
drizzle, the ruined landscape. I have tried to depict the handful of
significant characters that Riddley encounters, but I have left most
of the active moments of drama to him to recount.' QB

Cover artwork, *Waiting for Godot*, 2021

Pozzo's slave Lucky, carrying his bags.
Watercolour marker on watercolour paper

Vladimir and Estragon, fading at the end.
Watercolour marker on watercolour paper

In *Waiting for Godot* in 2021, Quentin drew more lonely figures on the road, going nowhere. In shades of purple, his stripped-down drawings harmonize with the play's severe yet humane blend of humour, desolation and hope. And with the elusive comedy of folk tale, in tune with Quentin's own surreal imagination.

Earlier illustrations of books had no influence when Quentin approached a classic text, except in two cases. The first was the invitation from the publisher Frederick Warne to celebrate Beatrix Potter's 150th anniversary in 2016, by illustrating the previously unpublished manuscript of *The Tale of Kitty-in-Boots*, for which she had never done any pictures. Despite some qualms, Quentin accepted at once, partly because she had once lived just around the corner from his London studio, in a house where Bousfield Primary School now stands, with which he had long been involved. Partly, too, because Kitty's friends call her 'Q', as his own friends call him. He could feel that the story of this elegant, well-behaved cat, who secretly nips out at night to go hunting, might almost have been left for him, 'and there was certainly more knockabout activity and airguns exploding than you would normally associate with our author.' The resulting drawings, in the traditional format, are uncanny cousins of the originals, yet recognizably his own.

Cover (left) and interior artwork, *The Tale of Kitty-in-Boots*, 2016

The second book, for Roger Thorp's new children's list at Thames & Hudson, was different in that, rather than keep a previous illustrator in mind, Quentin had to firmly turn his back. This was *The King of the Golden River*, John Ruskin's only children's book, the story of young Gluck's struggles against his two evil brothers, written for Effie Gray when she was twelve (later she and Ruskin would marry, briefly and unhappily). For many years Quentin had possessed a Victorian edition illustrated by Dicky Doyle, and it took time, and a greater

familiarity with Ruskin's 'passion for mountains, glaciers, weather', for him to overcome his respect for Doyle and set about it himself. Eventually, after carefully positioning his roughs in a cut-up text, Quentin plunged into drawing, feeling 'so positive and enthusiastic about the book that I was eager to imagine myself into the characters'. Finally the atmospheric watercolour was added. 'I felt very fortunate', he writes, 'that I had (at last) discovered that I had such an incomparable opportunity for illustration.'

Schwartz walking through the landscape, *The King of the Golden River*, 2019

6

Up the Wall

Public Spaces and Hospitals

Quentin's work has often leapt free of the page or the frame, climbing walls, swirling along corridors, and wrapping construction sites and grand old buildings. Many ventures have come from encounters with people who loved his drawings and felt that they could help to transform familiar settings, guiding people's expectations in a new and positive way. These large installations were made possible, too, by new techniques, above all by the magic of digital enlargement. As many galleries, schools and hospitals have shown over the years, for Quentin Blake a blank wall can be a very inviting canvas.

In 1999, when Quentin became Britain's first Children's Laureate, he wanted to use his platform to show children illustration alongside works of fine art. So he had the inspired idea of asking two or three art galleries if he could curate an exhibition for children that would include twenty-six paintings, arranged alphabetically. To his delight, Michael Wilson, director of exhibitions at the National Gallery, accepted enthusiastically, and when Quentin observed wryly that his own work 'would have no chance getting in alphabetically with either Bruegel or Botticelli as competition', Wilson suggested that he draw on the walls – every child's trespassing dream. So he did, although cheating slightly as the drawings were on acetate, which could be stripped off afterwards. Families could wander the gallery, guided by these black-and-white figures who chatter away about the everyday details they find in the pictures, like parcels or houses.

Quentin at work in the House of Illustration, 2014

Artwork for 'Tell Me a Picture', National Gallery, London, 2001. Pen and ink with watercolour halftone

It was a brilliant idea, allowing people to relate effortlessly to paintings, with the drawings removing anything daunting or intimidating from 'great art'. Over a quarter of a million visitors saw the show, 'some, I suspect and hope, who had perhaps never stepped inside the National Gallery before'.

Quentin went on to curate a similar show with Ghislaine Kenyon at the Petit Palais in Paris, the city's museum of fine arts. Titled 'Quentin Blake et les Demoiselles des Bords de Seine', it was based on the depiction of women in paintings in the gallery's reserve collection, which weren't usually seen, and the exhibition title came from a painting by Gustave Courbet in this collection. The walls were higher in this grand building, so he sketched ordinary children but gave them wings, like grubby cherubs. Sometimes his scenes illustrated smart goings-on, such as going to a party or taking a stroll – but in others the children simply climbed and flew, circling the pictures below.

En Societé and *La Promenade*, 'Quentin Blake et les Demoiselles des Bords de Seine', Petit Palais, Paris, 2005. Pen and ink with watercolour halftone

'Quentin Blake et les Demoiselles des Bords de Seine', Petit Palais, Paris, 2005

' This was all made possible by Gilles Chazal, the director of the
museum, who at our first meeting said, "carte blanche à Quentin
Blake." I particularly liked moments such as the one in this photo
where you get the original painting, the drawing on the wall and
the view outside.' **QB**

Soon the drawings jumped from inside to outside. A galaxy of characters in
red and black crowded on to a huge canvas that was wrapped around two sides
of the unsightly Stanley Building at King's Cross, London, in 2007, when the
new St Pancras station opposite had its royal opening. Drawn in the studio by
hand and then re-created digitally on a huge scale, the scene was a celebration
of music, art and jollity – a 'welcoming committee' of Londoners young and
old, out on the town.

In a less riotous but still irreverent mood, Quentin undertook a commission
from the University of Cambridge, where he had been a student many years

before, to produce artworks to celebrate its 800th anniversary. For this he settled on what he called an 'Informal Panorama' (often very informal indeed), showing famous figures from the university's past, and poking fun at them in passing. Once drawn, the pictures could be printed in vastly different sizes from a Christmas card to a huge banner, seventy feet long, hiding scaffolding in front of King's College.

Above: All wrapped up, the Stanley Building, London, 2007
Overleaf: Artwork for the wrap of the Stanley Building, 2007. Pen and ink with watercolour halftone

Cambridge 800: A Cambridge Panorama, 2009

Art can transform a building, a street, a famous view. But it can also transform intimate surroundings, bringing personal consolation or comfort, or heartening encouragement at critical times. Quentin's work over the years with The Nightingale Project, a charity which specializes in mental health, based at the Central and North West London NHS Foundation Trust, is an embodiment of his belief in the transformative power of art. His first work with them, in 2006–7, was a series of paintings to brighten the dull walls of the Kershaw Ward, a mental-health centre for older patients in the Kensington & Chelsea Mental Health Centre. In the corridor, jubilant images show cavorting pensioners, balancing and swinging in high branches. Trees, Quentin notes, give a decorative format perfect for a flat wall, but one that leaves room for a whole range of activities: 'it's a mise-en-scène that allows both comforting situations, on platforms and in hammocks, as well as nervous wobbly ones. The fundamental idea, of course, is that if you jump (or fall) out of the trees there is always someone there to catch you.' The portraits of all the characters are compassionate and whimsical but acutely observed

Artwork for the Kershaw Ward, Kensington & Chelsea Mental Health Centre, London, 2006.
Also published in *You're Only Young Twice*, 2008

Artwork for the Kershaw Ward, Kensington & Chelsea Mental Health Centre, London, 2006.
Also published in *You're Only Young Twice*, 2008

and unsentimental. Oddity is welcomed, infirmity irrelevant, old and young
play together – often noisily, like the madly grinning drummer and small boy.
Stories, too, hang in the balance: will the man with the beard stay up in the
fork of the branch, or will he crash down on the table of drinks below? Will
the tightrope-walking girl land on the easel – or the hat?

After the Kershaw Ward corridor, he made drawings in a variety of forms
and media that were reproduced as prints for the bedrooms. Several included
cats or birds 'some of which came out looking as though they might have psy-
chological problems of their own'. More Nightingale collaborations followed.
For elderly mental-health patients at Northwick Park Hospital in Harrow,
Quentin invented *Our Friends in the Circus*, an exuberant if perilous defiance
of age and gravity, in all senses, a reminder that however odd they look, old
people still have 'skills honed over the years, still fluent and functioning'. At
the Gordon Hospital in Westminster, folk swim underwater, lost to daily life,
yet still very much themselves, in their own coats and clothes, not at all both-
ered by their translation to their odd state in this new realm.

20   21

22   23

Our Friends in the Circus, Northwick Park Hospital, London, 2008

In London's Vincent Square Clinic (another Nightingale project) Quentin talked to patients at the Eating Disorder Service, a lively, clever, self-aware bunch of young people, although several were heartbreakingly ill. It would be fine for him to draw anything, they said, while admitting that food was a problematic issue. Deciding not to avoid it, but setting aside any metaphorical significance, he drew scenes where food was an easy part of daily life, 'maybe even crumbs for the birds'. His patients felt they saw themselves in a mirror, not criticized or judged, but accepted with an easy goodwill.

Opposite and above: *Life Under Water*, Gordon Hospital, London, 2008. Giclee prints

' In some of the hospital drawings I made use
of fantasy, to help people imagine they can do
things which they actually can't at the moment.
The situation here is the opposite. These
patients have enough fantasy about their own
selves so that I thought it was appropriate
to be realistic and offer pictures of ordinary
everyday life in what I hoped would be
a reassuring way.' **QB**

Ordinary Life, Vincent Square Eating Disorder Service, 2011.
From the top: *Self-portrait*, *In the Garden* and *Daz the Dog*

Welcome to Planet Zog, Alexandra Avenue Health & Social Care Unit, London, 2007

Quentin's prints have cheered up patients of all ages in many hospitals, both in the UK and in France. In Paris at the Hôpital Armand Trousseau, where many children came from immigrant African families, he drew children from different backgrounds exploring life high up in the trees, sometimes wobbly and precarious but always with someone nearby to help. For the Alexandra Avenue Health & Social Care Unit, a London centre for children and young people, he created Planet Zog, a place where stalk-eyed creatures stick out spotty tongues and green consultants scribble notes. He was, he said, just showing people 'in strange situations which they are more or less coping with'. The pictures made them smile and think that 'aliens' – even doctors – might not be so threatening after all.

In hospitals people often have to cope with a situation that seems unbearable. Quentin never makes light of their plight. Instead he gives them something that recognizes their distress but offers something to hang on to. At the

The Dragon Centre, St George's Hospital, London, 2014

Dragon Centre for children at St George's Hospital in Tooting, this comical comfort returns in the shape of – what else? – a dragon, who has to come to terms with hospital life too.

In one hospital department the mood is different – the maternity unit. Although tension and apprehension are present, and sometimes tragedy, the dominant feeling is one of hope and celebration. When he was invited to decorate a new wing of the maternity unit at Angers University Hospital in France, Quentin used a swimming theme: women surrounded by rococo swirls of seaweed floated along the corridor and appeared with shoals of

Corridor window in the maternity unit, Angers University Hospital, 2011

fish in prints for individual delivery suites. The project was, he wrote in *Beyond the Page*, 'one of the most gratifying I have ever been engaged on'.

The watery scheme is not merely a reminder of the amniotic fluid or of the way that newborn babies swim naturally, but a way of imparting movement and freedom, the feeling, while in labour, that 'something is just around the corner.' It also has an air of mystery, as if at this vital moment women enter another element. Mothers and children swim together along the corridor walls and even on the windows, serene against the sky. In creating these artworks, Quentin was guided by the words of the hospital director: 'The important thing is the exchange of look between the mother and the baby.' The tender, vital moment of contact found its way too on to the walls of the new birth centre at Rosie Hospital, in Cambridge – swimming mothers, with babies floating, falling, swooping and flying into life.

Delivery suite artwork, Angers University Hospital, 2011. Reed pen, ink and watercolour

Artwork for the Rosie Birth Centre, Cambridge, 2012. Reed pen, ink and watercolour

7

Solo Sequences

Personal Series: for exhibitions

Over the years Quentin Blake has frequently made drawings, prints and watercolours that fall into sequences, some with only a handful of individual drawings, others as many as sixty. These series have often formed the basis for exhibitions on particular themes, although they constantly defy easy categories.

They are drawn or painted in a mode quite different from his illustrations, as if a stream was bubbling up from a deep level. When Claudia Zeff, editor of his book *A Year of Drawings*, asked him how these 'families' of works came about, he replied that although they don't illustrate a narrative, 'for me there is still a story in them. I like to explore the different possibilities of some relationship or someone's behaviour. Whether I am inventing a set of situations or working to an existing story, the business is one of imagination. I suppose where no story exists, I am implying that there is one somewhere.'

An early example of such a series, shown in Mel Calman's London gallery in the 1970s, formed the exhibition 'Arrows of Love' at the House of Illustration almost fifty years later in 2018. Graphically expressive in their purity of line, the drawings all have a comedic touch, while suggesting that 'love' is not always comforting, or safe, for a woman. However much they crouch, or dodge, or lean, or run, the arrows still find them (the title originally applied to this group was *St Valentine's Day Massacre*).

Women & Creatures, exhibited as 'Nos Compagnons',
Galerie Martine Gossieaux, Paris, 2014

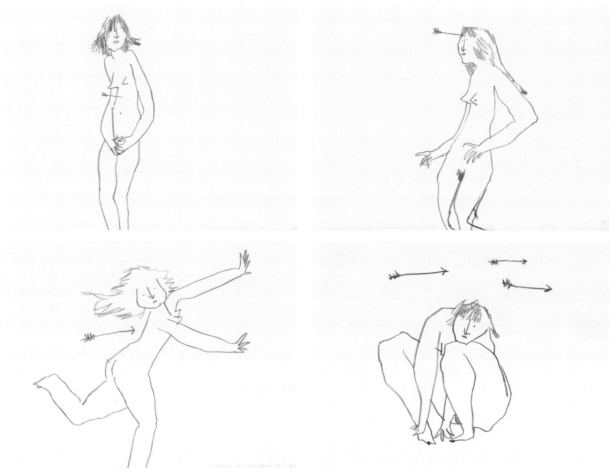

St Valentine's Day Massacre, c. 1975, exhibited as 'Arrows of Love', House of Illustration, London, 2018.
Pencil on watercolour paper

Quentin is superb at creating small dramas. Often, as he draws, he says he does not know quite what to expect. And sometimes his subjects look equally uncertain. In an exhibition at the Marlborough Gallery in London in 2012 he called them *Characters in Search of a Story*. They wait, poised, as if it is up to us to provide them with the answer – a three-way conversation between artist, subject and viewer.

The *Character* drawings are large, with a minimal landscape or setting. Another series, *Companions*, shows pairs of figures, hinting at a relationship, accompanied by a slight sense of unease. By contrast, in *Old and Young*, where the gold of youth springs out against the pallor of the old, the people are genuinely 'companionable', passing on knowledge, sharing interests and affection.

Top: *Characters in Search of a Story*, 2012. China marker on watercolour paper
Above: *Companions*, 2012. China marker on watercolour paper

Old and Young, 2012. Pen, coloured ink and
watercolour on watercolour paper

Sporting Women, 2011. Stabilo watercolour pastels, on watercolour paper

The energy that flows through these drawings bursts out in the same exhibition in the strong, athletic *Sporting Women*, drawn in vibrant watercolour pencil that renders their powerful limbs radiant. They seem almost like woad-painted warriors from a distant age, fizzing with power, ready for anything, with no need to wait for a story.

40 Women for Downing, 2020. Oil pastel on drawing-book paper

A different kind of female strength, intellectual rather than physical, looks out from a series made to celebrate the 40th anniversary of women being admitted to his old college, Downing College in Cambridge. (When he was there, he says, 'it was very much a male college'.) In the series *40 Women for Downing*, the imaginary female students - one to mark each year - are strong, serious, positive, full of inner thought. He found it fascinating, he says, to try to create different variations of character, and went on afterwards to build a whole series of 'Imaginary Portraits'.

To offset any sense of seriousness, with the Downing portraits he also showed some drawings in pencil and ballpoint pen called *Wayward Locks*, a fantasia of wild and decorative hairdressing.

'One of the advantages of hair in drawings is that it will stay where
you put it, which gives you the possibility of all kinds of arrangements
that you might find difficult in real life… What is interesting to me is
the feeling that the hair has done that itself – nobody has dressed
their hair to be like that, it came like that – it's a sort of expression
of their imagination.' **QB**

Wayward Locks, 2018. Ballpoint pen in A4 drawing books

Women with Birds, 2012. Etching

His exhibitions often contain similar sudden shifts of register. 'Contrasts of mood and medium', he explains, 'were very clear in the Marlborough Gallery in 2012, where the colourful athletes hung alongside the *Characters in Search of a Story*'. Another contrast was provided by a set of etchings of *Women with Birds*. Here, the sharper lines give a crisp sense of confidence. The nude with her topknot and bow, for example, completely sure in her handling of the docile crow, is both elegant and witty - like a small, unexpected poem.

Close links between people, birds, animals and fantastical creatures often appear. One series, drawn over several years, became the exhibition 'Nos Compagnons' at the Galerie Martine Gossieaux in Paris in 2014. Among the sequences, *Women & Creatures*, drawn in pen, ink and watercolour, was particularly tender. One feels that they care for each other. The women's nakedness expresses their total ease in this imaginary animal world.

' One of the attractions of drawing
   is that it lends itself easily to metaphor
   – so you might think of these beings,
   even though scaly or hairy, as pets,
   children, brothers, boyfriends, perhaps
   even husbands. You will know best.' QB

Women & Creatures, exhibited as 'Nos Compagnons',
Galerie Martine Gossieaux, Paris, 2014

Children with Birds & Dogs, 2019. Oil pastel on watercolour paper

'The drawings look at the relationship of the children
I draw with living things around them – sometimes
positive but often tentative – comparable to the
relationships [real children] may have with the world
around them. I hope they invite our sympathy but also
our respect.' **QB**

A feeling of companionship between beings with very different experience of the world also imbues *Children with Birds & Dogs*, drawn for the Foundling Museum in 2019. Focusing on the emotional life of childhood, the Museum asked several writers, including Michael Rosen, Opefoluwa Sarah Adegbite and Jackie Kay, to write poems and stories inspired by the drawings. To find a heron walking alongside you down a stream or across a field may be unlikely, but imagination can create such alliances: for a solitary child, a fantastical friend may be an essential guide to a rich inner life.

An even closer fusion of human and other forms of life is imagined in a set of etchings simply called *Insects*, subtly translating activity from one realm to another. Is this an ant, or is it an old lady dropping her bag because she is so keen on reading her many books (useful to have an abundance of legs)? Are these two figures insects at all, or an immediately recognisable, gentle but harassed mother, dragging her reluctant child shopping or to school? Somehow, by using a different species, Quentin can show graphically what it means to be 'a person'.

Insects, 2012. Etching with aquatint

Unicyclist, 2015. Brush, ink and watercolour on watercolour paper

The insects made people laugh, as well as ponder. So did the exhibition 'Life Under Water', shown at the Jerwood Gallery (now Hastings Contemporary) in 2015. Quentin has owned a house in Hastings Old Town for more than forty years and since it opened as the Jerwood Gallery in 2012, he has been closely involved with Hastings Contemporary, the beautiful modern gallery facing the grey waves of the English Channel. His collaboration with its director, Liz Gilmore, began with an exhibition called 'Artists on the Beach' to accompany the gallery's summer drawing festival in 2014, and since then, as the gallery's first Artist Patron, he has often shown his work there. The gallery's sympathetic atmosphere has proved so important that even now,

Morris Dancers, 2015. Brush, ink and watercolour on watercolour paper

he says, when 'perhaps one ought to be retiring or something, I think I'm doing more drawings than ever, with Hastings in mind.' At ninety, he shows no inclination to retire.

In 'Life Under Water' he adopted a theme of some of his hospital drawings, showing people swimming in their everyday clothes, garlanded with fish and seaweed. In the hospitals, he had hoped this might suggest 'individuals finding themselves in a physically and psychologically strange situation'. In Hastings, as he wrote at the time, in a coda to Ghislaine Kenyon's book, his twenty-four pictures became a way of depicting, and enjoying, 'specific Hastings types (and in Hastings, of course, the fish are everywhere).

So there are holidaymakers, schoolchildren, middle-aged ladies, the pur-
chasers of antiques and second-hand books – but also characters with
the urge to dress up that Hastings seems to inspire: bikers, pirates, morris
dancers, Jack o' the Green.' It was a way for Quentin, and for the gallery,
to acknowledge the lively mix of the town, and to salute it.

In Hastings Quentin also contributed a vividly coloured wall-hanging for
the newly refurbished Children's Library, with an old fishing boat in the fore-
ground. Against a rosy sky a host of children fly high, reading their books, as
they do in a similar decoration for the French Institute in South Kensington.

More surreal flights came to Hastings in 'The World of Hats' in 2018, an
exhibition that he calls modestly 'a fantastical exploration of headgear in a
variety of sizes and media'. He began by thinking forty drawings would fill the
space well, but once started, he became so caught up 'that whenever I felt like

Pirate Drummer, 2015. Brush, ink and watercolour on watercolour paper

drawing something it turned out to be another hat. While I was at work on the series I also discovered Winsor & Newton watercolour markers, which gave me an extra motive for experimenting with them. By the time I persuaded myself to stop I found I had a collection of over a hundred drawings.' Briefly, hats were an obsession – and his enjoyment of their potential is obvious and infectious.

> ' All sorts of objects and activities appear on the hats, and I am often not quite sure if the wearers are aware of them. Perhaps the most interesting hats for me are those where yet another face appears – it's almost like seeing a mask and the face behind it at the same time. I came to feel eventually that the hats have taken on a sort of life of their own.' QB

Hats, 2017. Coloured ink on watercolour paper

Above and opposite: *Hand in Hand*, 2021

The hats are more than headgear. Each is a small character study, often featuring Quentin's familiar creatures with spiky hair and long beaks and noses. The wearer may be unaware of them but the hat-beings feel like avatars, a frivolous eruption of the subconscious, hinting at hidden fears, desires and pleasures. Like all the 'solo sequences', they are a guide to who we are.

In Hastings, in May 2021, Quentin added some new drawings to a sombre exhibition, 'We Live in Worrying Times'. These extra pen-and-ink sketches formed a sequence he called *Hand in Hand*, a group full of a rush of life. These drawings speak without words. Like the hats, so wickedly energizing, they suggest that we all have a daring imagination somewhere in our heads, a capacity for joy. And as long as we can do things together, hand in hand, hope is not lost, even in the darkest times.

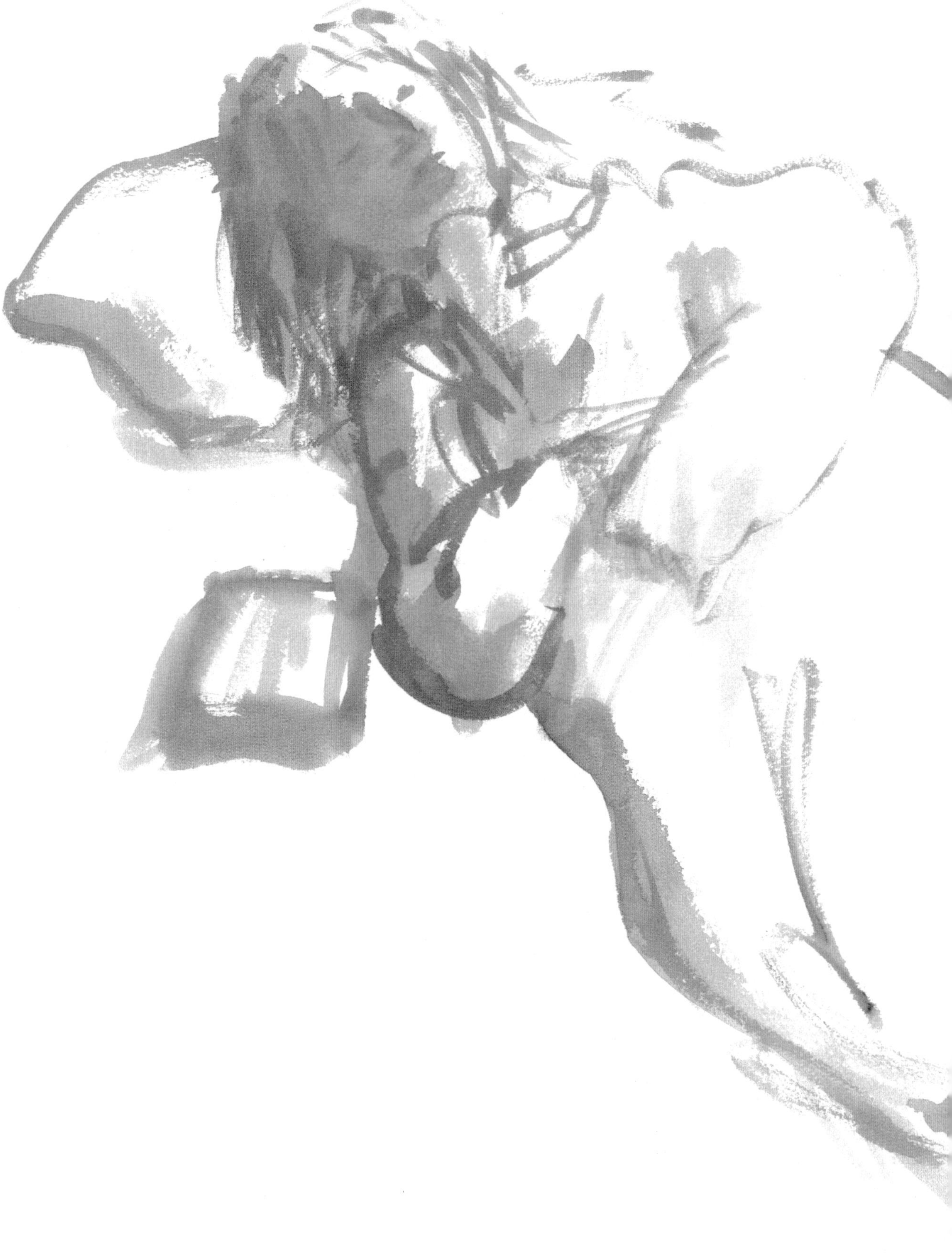

8

Twilight and Sunlight

Personal Series: from book to gallery and back

Several other sets of drawings, often related to exhibitions, have found their way into books. The mood of these sequences varies from quiet to rumbustious, from easy to harsh, skirting perilous depths and emerging into light again. They reflect Quentin's curiosity and passing preoccupations, and his deeper interests and concerns, but also his love of books themselves and his fascination with the processes of reading and imagining – how stories and ideas and characters get into our minds and linger in our memory.

One early set became the volume *Woman with a Book* in 1999. In romantic watercolour images, Quentin explored the absorption of the reader, even when the book is not in her hand but lying by her side: his women have the wondering, far-away look of someone who has been transported to another land or life. As Russell Hoban noted in his introduction (which he called 'Wrapped Attention, Also Unwrapped'), under their dressing gowns and blankets the rapt readers are female nudes. Quentin later explained that the idea had developed when he decided, after he showed an exhibition of nudes in 1993, that just for a change, they should be covered: 'I think I had some undefined notion that their being more or less wrapped corresponded somehow to areas of privacy or introspection.' There is also something sexy in their relaxed poses, in the sense of safety, of being held warmly as they read – all this contributes to the sense of dreamy comfort and escape, and the way their life seems to flow beyond the page.

Preceding pages, above and opposite: *Woman with a Book*, 1999

' I discovered that the women were reading, that their
attention was elsewhere, that they were no longer conscious
of being turned into art objects… They were also becoming
more like individuals, reacting differently to their reading;
or perhaps the way they read is indicative of some other
situation they're in.' QB

Constant Readers, QB Papers, 2019

' Even in the age of the iPad and the smartphone, books offer
   things that they cannot. Not the text, of course, but the physical
   presence – the look, the feel, the smell.' **QB**

Reading is a recurring theme of Quentin's work, from the dreaming women
to the children flying high with their books in his murals for libraries and
schools. In *Constant Readers*, in 2019, he drew book-addicts who carry their
tomes with them everywhere. In an interview for *Country Life* that year, he
admitted that 'it's the ordinary readers, so to speak, who are the most fascinating to me and the ones I most want to draw - the little theatre of their gestures
and reactions, the positions they get themselves into, their expressions of

doubt, apprehension, excitement and delight… but I couldn't deprive myself also of the sight of sheer boredom.' Some of his readers, however, cling to the words, even when high winds ruffle the pages and whirl away the scarves around their necks.

Constant Readers became one of twenty large-format books published under the umbrella of 'The QB Papers'. These were all drawn over the space of a few months in 2019, apart from *Thirteen Things You Cannot Really Manage Without*, which started life as *Objects* for an exhibition in Aldeburgh in 2018, and *Scenes at Twilight*, which were shown in their original colours in Hastings the same year. They were all printed at once and issued in four tranches between August 2019 and July 2020. Several other delicious groups, ranging from *Optimistic Suitors* to *In Praise of Potted Plants*, which 'may not find their way into print' have been included in the section of Quentin's website called 'Every Other Friday'.

A selection of the QB Papers, 2019

Feet in the Water, QB Papers, 2019

Quentin's interest in drawing *Feet in the Water* came from paddling himself, either at Hastings or on the Atlantic coast in France: 'I think we all want to have the pleasure of seeing the reflections in the water and to share in the experience.' These drawings are relatively naturalistic, asking us to share the enjoyment. Quentin's humorous observation also comes to the fore in a sequence showing twenty bald men, 'in differing modes of thought'. These are comical, in the way of an old joke, but the baldness also lets Quentin investigate the shape of the head, the skull beneath the skin, and somehow makes the features stand out so that the expression, the quizzical act of thinking itself, becomes the real subject.

20 Bald Men, QB Papers, 2020. Pen and ink on watercolour paper

' I drew all these in bed one morning. I'm not sure why I chose this kind of person, but once again the interest for me is in the variations on a fixed set of features: bald head, spectacles, moustache.' **QB**

Some QB Papers, like the serendipitous, and often perilous, meetings in *Chance Encounters*, spin into fantasy, while offering a short visual essay on balance. This sequence moves towards themes that have run increasingly through Quentin's work in recent years, particularly people and creatures on the move, at dusk or in the dark. They are present too in another QB Paper, *Riders by Night*, where he created a moonlit array of landscapes and creatures, among them the magnificent and ghostly owl with his shock-haired rider.

Chance Encounters, QB Papers, 2020   *Riders by Night*, QB Papers, 2019

The Language of the Fan, QB Papers, 2020. Watercolour pencil on watercolour paper

In other QB booklets, the effect is very different. It can be playful and elegant, as in the balletic line drawings of *The Language of the Fan*, or comically ludicrous, as in the responses of people in *The Mouse on a Tricycle*. Other sets of drawings are inventively absurd, like the woman balancing a banana on her nose in *Thirteen Things You Cannot Really Manage Without*.

'Heaven knows how I thought of a mouse on a tricycle! It's just
there in one of my notebooks somewhere. Of course, the point
is not it, but the range of reactions of the onlookers.' **QB**

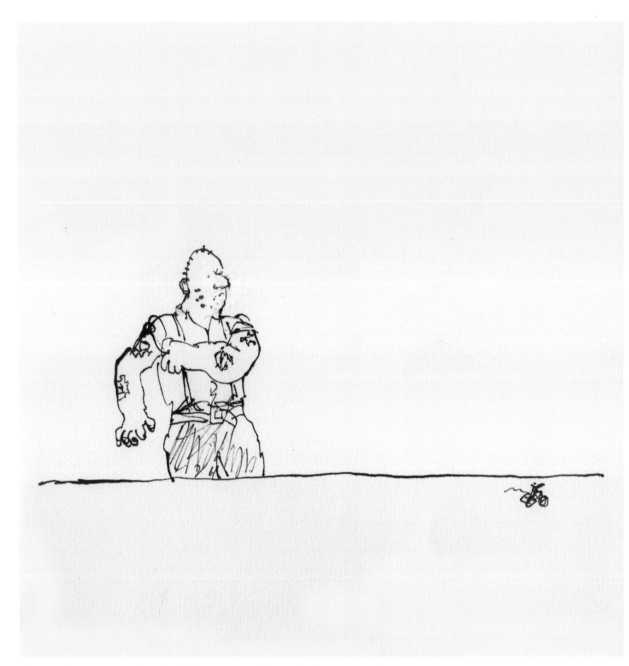

Above: *The Mouse on a Tricycle*, QB Papers, 2019. Pen and ink on watercolour paper
Opposite: *Thirteen Things You Cannot Really Manage Without*, QB Papers, 2020.
Pen and ink on watercolour paper

Banana

All the QB Papers are short entertainments, like revues, or cabarets. And all display an amused delight in the act of drawing itself, reflected in the determination of the *Wildlife Artists of the Year*, constantly challenged or frustrated by their subjects. In each set, too, Quentin uses different styles and techniques appropriate to his subject, from eerily atmospheric combinations of ink and watercolour to the delicacy of a watercolour wash. And when he uses a pen alone, with sure hand, he can demonstrate the bravura power of a simple - or not so simple - line.

'A set of drawings showing the interaction between Man and a Line on the Floor.' **QB**

Above, left: *Wildlife Artists of the Year*, QB Papers, 2020
Above, right: *Linear*, QB Papers, 2020. Pen and ink on watercolour paper

In an exhibition in Hastings in 2017, 'The Only Way to Travel', Quentin developed a lyrical imagery that would feature in several books. In pen-and-ink drawings and watercolours, small, scumbled figures trek across wild landscapes. Others sail over rocky peaks in a cavalcade of animal-based transports that rival Heath Robinson's mad inventions. He explains in his book *Pens, Ink and Places* that these 'new and unexpected' modes of travel had evolved in part from drawings he had made over the last few years for his friend Linda Kitson, who had been his pupil and then his colleague at the Royal College of Art. 'We called them *Vehicles of the Mind*,' he writes, 'and they were drawn on a variety of sketchbook pages, notebooks, paper napkins. Each was a variation on the same formula: a large, frequently angst-ridden visage, and in a driving seat behind it a fairly relaxed-looking driver – ladies of various ages, or a formal-looking gentleman.... The game was to vary the elements on each occasion – the degree of comfort or distress, the number of legs or wheels or feet or wings.'

Vehicles of the Mind, 2009. Fibre-tip pen

In the show in 2017 this variety continued. In one large drawing (five by four feet) a rider zooms ahead on a thickly sketched scooter. In another of the same size a man teeters on a tightrope, shouldering a pile of luggage and a stray friend, and leading an obedient dog. In the most exuberant, sketchy sketch of all, children wave from the jagged back of a dragon on wheels.

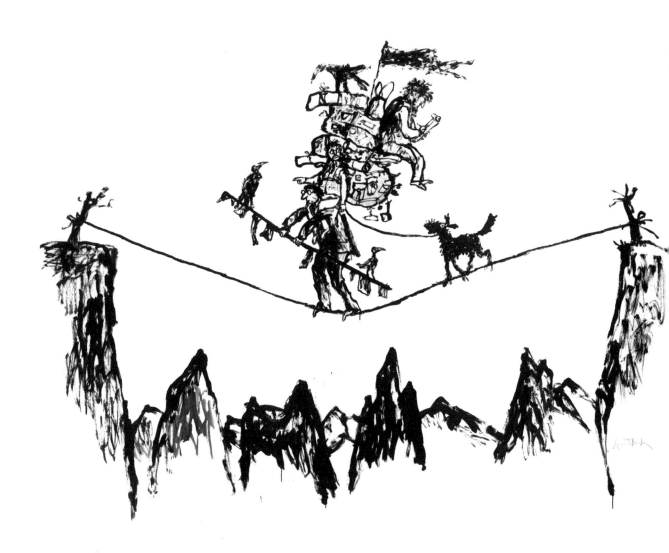

The Only Way to Travel, 2017. Brush, rollers and acrylic on photographer's paper

The Only Way to Travel, 2017. Brush and acrylic on watercolour paper

In 2018 one set of watercolours shown in this exhibition, some re-envisioned in horizontal form, became the book *Moonlight Travellers*, for which Will Self wrote a haunting text. In these the modes of transport are still more bizarre, from a flying-fish plane with spindly wheel-legs to a gyrocopter that looks like a smug and sleepy turtle, or a flag-bedecked two-storey trolley, moved by heaving on a pole.

It's noticeable, however, that all these travellers on their weird machines seemed to move only by night beneath the green, or gold, or red, or purple moon.

Above and opposite: *Moonlight Travellers* shown in the exhibition
'The Only Way to Travel', Hastings Contemporary, 2017

Opposite and above: *Moonlight Travellers*, 2018

In 2020 Quentin picked up this thread again, this time as *Vélos Tout Terrain*, with more vehicles making their spindly way across moor and heath and mountain.

Above and opposite: *Vélos Tout Terrain*, 2020

The twilit and moonlit sketches are full of macabre sensations and eerie suspense, giving one a sense of being carried into a world on the edges of dream. In 2019 Quentin created the QB Paper *Scenes at Twilight*, and he revisited this dusky world yet again in a new series, *Seen at Twilight*, in 2020. These rough-looking ink sketches with their vivid watercolour washes moved even further into a world of unexplained travel, becoming ever more mysterious. There is a story in the figures hovering on the shore, crossing an abyss on a tightrope among the birds, dashing with their pram down a hill, and struggling through grey, still waters among the rocks. But it is a story we must create ourselves.

Above, opposite and overleaf: *Seen at Twilight*, 2020

In 2020-1, during the long months of lockdown, Quentin drew continually. Many of these works were selected for *A Year of Drawings*, an array of separate sequences, tender and odd, scary and fanciful. The travellers of *Seen at Twilight* appear here, and so do the wondrous vehicles of the moonlight travellers.

Sometimes, the journey seems almost impossible. Danger is present, both in the terrain and in daunting, unstable structures, summoned up in drawings of high places, with no ground visible beneath the traveller's feet, only a bridge made of a wobbly tree branch or scaffolding ruled by a set of unreadable instructions.

Above and opposite: *High Places*, 2021

In late 2020, however, feeling that he had lingered in the dusk and dark long enough, and that perhaps people would like something more cheery, Quentin drew a new sequence, leading his travellers out into the sun.

A golden sun, haloed in red, beams from the corner of the page on to the familiar many-legged machines, but also, in one drawing, on to a hatted man with a pole, steering a primitive canoe shared with a family of cranes. Under sunshades and canopies, the mood is sunlit and sociable. This is a time to enjoy, to read a book or listen to a story, to move and feel alive, wheeling high above the stream or floating downriver while trees wave above. As Quentin acknowledged, 'in challenging times humour can be the best tonic.'

Above and opposite: *Sunshine Travellers*, 2020

9

Worrying Times
Some Feeling of Sympathy

Images from one show or book often morph into others, accumulating meaning and power. In one watercolour in 'The Only Way to Travel' in 2017, a trail of tired walkers march on and on, under a huge purple moon. These travellers and their companions flowed on into the dreamlike pictures of *Moonlight Travellers*, and then merged with darker imaginings of people fleeing for shelter in whatever way they can.

So where might these travellers end up? In 2021 Quentin created a new series called *On the Beach*. This has nothing to do with families rushing to the seaside, children cavorting on the sand, or fishing boats drawn up on Hastings' pebbles. In these works the beach is an anonymous liminal space, a place of departure, a shore of arrival. Drawn in pen and ink, with a watercolour wash that bleeds into the paper like rain, the sketches show moments of anxiety or hope, shared by weary travellers. In 2020 and 2021 thousands of migrants crossed the Channel in fragile inflatables, landing on Britain's southern shore. Although Quentin's pictures make no direct reference to their plight, they inevitably come to mind. His travellers could be any one of us, joining a continuing journey through life, not always easy to bear. It's no surprise that, as well as Greenpeace and many medical, educational and environmental charities, he has given work to support Freedom from Torture, Shelter and Survival International.

Stone Heads, series 2, 2018. Fibre-tip pen in a drawing book

The Only Way to Travel, 2017

On the Beach, 2020

Long before the Covid-19 pandemic, the world had its share of afflictions. Explosions were ripping through Syrian villages, floods in Asia and droughts in Africa were driving people from their homes, refugees from oppression, terror and torture were streaming across borders. In the Mediterranean, refugees drowned as they tried to reach Europe. Men, women and children, desperate to reach British shores, huddled in Calais camps, rushed into lorries, clung to frail boats. In the streets of the country they were aiming for, homeless people sheltered in doorways and families relied on foodbanks. Quentin was aware of this from the news but saw it happening with what, he says, felt like a certain detachment. His real feelings began to appear only when he started to paint.

He was prompted, as so often, by a story, which he tells vividly in a video showing him with a large plate of black acrylic paint and a long, thick brush, setting about painting a huge mural on the wall of Hastings Contemporary. A couple of years before, he explains, he had ordered a taxi. And then 'rather to my surprise the taxi driver got in as well, and sat opposite me and said "we live in worrying times". The driver went on to say that he'd seen Picasso's *Guernica* – the huge painting from 1937 of the bombing of a village during the Spanish Civil War – a couple of times in Spain. And he said, "what we need is something like that for our own times. And you're the person to do it."'

> So I said, 'Well, it's not quite my kind of thing, is it?
> And he said, 'Yes, you're the man…. Cometh the hour, cometh the man'
> So I said, 'Well, I'll see what I can do…'

What he could do turned out to be *The Taxi Driver*, a thirty-foot mural in harsh black and white, stretching across the gallery. The experience of painting this was quite new, different from anything he had attempted before – it would not be an enlargement of a small drawing, but painted directly on the wall. In his late eighties Quentin's sight showed some signs of deterioration, and to draw at the size that he had done for years was becoming more difficult; sometimes he had to resort to a magnifying glass. Subsequently, drawing on the wall had a special attraction for him. He says, 'I really ought to be drawing at this size all the time.'

Quentin painting *The Taxi Driver* mural, 2020

So he started in the way that western readers read a page, beginning on the left, with a cloud of planes and drones, and working to the right, following the story as it unfolds. Refugees straggle on, taking shelter, carrying burdens, caring for children, trailing across a war-blasted landscape. It was finished in a single day. High up in one corner is the taxi, 'in the distance, with nowhere to go'. The encounter came increasingly to feel like a dream. He had asked for the driver's name, but was told that there was no need, 'as I keep an eye on everything anyway'. No deity here, no spirit from beyond, but an everyday conscience, transporting us all.

' We need art because it's got life in it… you may be drawing
a very distressing thing… but what I hope is that it's not entirely
distressing, because the way you present it, the way it's drawn,
has got something enhancing in it. So that no matter how grisly
it is, the fact that there is drawing in it means you are embracing
it, you're moving forward, you're doing something with it, and
that something is very fascinating. For me it's drawing, but it's
true of all the arts and that is why we need them.' **QB**

Quentin can be fierce and satirical. He could have attacked the corrupt
politicians, the arms dealers and torturers. But that wasn't his aim. Instead
he wanted to show fellow feeling, to acknowledge people across the world
who are suffering and in distress.

'We Live in Worrying Times' was due to open before Easter, in April 2020.
Then the lockdowns hit. All was not lost, as the show took a digital form with
a robot named Double, made up of a video screen and a camera on wheels
(a collaboration between the gallery, the D4D Project, Accentuate and Bristol

The Taxi Driver, 2020, Hastings Contemporary. Acrylic paint on paper

Robotics Lab) guiding viewers around the gallery – appropriately absurd yet functional. The first people to see *The Taxi Driver* in person came in August that year, by which time it seemed even more relevant.

The wanderers in the bleak landscape of the mural walked on in the series of illustrations for Michael Rosen's book of poems about migration, *On the Move*. 'Migration is the story of the human race,' writes Rosen. 'Everyone comes from somewhere/ Everyone has a past.' All through history wars and famines and persecution have driven people from their homes, escaping on foot or in carts and now in cars and trains, lorries and boats. Quentin's drawings show shawled mothers and gaunt fathers creating makeshift beds for their children, wading across swamps, crowding into fragile craft – looking for safety and a better life.

On the Move: Poems about Migration, 2020

From figures in the distance, he moved to close-ups, drawing a series of portraits in crayon and pencil, ballpoint pen and fibre-tip pen, of anxious people, men, women, couples, a mother and child. These formed groups of *The Perplexed, Something Wrong Somewhere, Apprehensive Girls and Women,* and *Unfortunates*. All their stories are withheld – 'we don't know what they are anxious about' – but a portrait, Quentin thinks, allows an artist – and a viewer – to feel in contact with what people are thinking or feeling. The emotion shows in the face, and if you catch that, all the nuances of feeling carry you on. This is also the secret of his illustration for children's books, where a facial expression can tell so much: bafflement, delight, alarm. Getting that expression was the most difficult thing, he remembers, and he would always tackle this first, using his technique of putting paper over the outline drawing

On the Move: Poems about Migration, 2020

The Perplexed, 2020. Chinagraph pencil in a drawing book

on the lightbox and drawing it again. This meant that if it was wrong, he could always throw it away. Many sessions, he says wryly, ended with him 'surrounded by expensive sheets of watercolour, with a small face bearing not quite the right expression in the middle of each'.

Whether drawn in pencil, oil pastel or ballpoint pen, these drawings are oddly beautiful. As Quentin himself says, the eyes, as in so much of his work, are mere dots, a way of reminding us that these people are fictional, and giving us distance. But those dots are powerfully expressive. We can see that there is indeed something wrong.

' Here what I hope is that the oil pastel has some of the blur of
reality, almost as though it might have been done from life.' QB

Apprehensive Girls and Women, 2020. Oil pastel in a drawing book

Unfortunates, 2020. Chinagraph pencil in a drawing book

Two years before this series of troubled souls, Quentin had searched for the way that a head can express the essence of feeling in a strange sequence of *Stone Heads*. Stranded in an open landscape, severed from their bodies, these heads appear huge. They feel like great symbolic figures, or toppled idols.

Even more powerful, in their rugged, awful simplicity, is the series *Eroded Heads*, their eyes near the top, their features eaten away by time, or war, or wind and weather and devastation. These too appeared, with the *Stone Heads*, in 'We Live in Worrying Times'. Like the anxious people, they wring our hearts. In all the works in this exhibition, Quentin says, 'I hope there will be some feeling of sympathy there... I'm not sure what feeling I want to elicit for them, but I do feel there should be *some* feeling for other people, even though they are stones, or eroded, or something like that.' They ask us to recognize others, however greatly their lives and predicaments differ from our own: 'they are other identities... they have feelings and distresses.' Once we see this, we can begin to be together in the world.

Something Wrong Somewhere, 2020. Ballpoint pen in a drawing book

' The stone heads are like Easter Island heads…
they stand in open landscapes… The curious thing
for me, and I don't know how I arrived at it, is
that they have emotions… You're not expected
to know how they got there, or why they're there
– it's another range of experience going on.' QB

Stone Heads, series 2, 2018. Fibre-tip pen in a drawing book

10

Imaginary Portraits
Discovery through Drawing

Afeter finishing *40 Women for Downing*, the series of imaginary women students, Quentin felt the urge to continue drawing portraits, working not from life but from a mix of memory and imagination and long-honed skill. Inspired by his exhibition 'Children with Birds & Dogs' at the Foundling Museum in 2019, for example, he drew touching individual portraits of children, suggestive of the innocence of childhood, yet hinting at a hidden, harder life.

The imaginary portraits are quite different from Quentin's illustrative work. 'Illustration,' he says, 'or at any rate illustration the way I do it, has marked affinities with acting. The facial expression, the pose, the gesture, all help to express a moment of narrative, or to imply such moment if no narrative exists. I mention this simply to emphasize the fact that my imaginary portraits have no relation to this at all; they refer outside themselves only in some particular temporary facial reaction.'

During the lockdowns of 2020 and 2021, an intense period of drawing fitted the more solitary life that Quentin, like so many of us, lived. As Claudia Zeff explains in her introduction to *A Year of Drawings*, 'In normal times, he would make two daily trips to his office across the square where he lives – one in the morning and one in the afternoon – to see what business there was for him to

Young Faces, 2019. Chinagraph pencil on watercolour paper

deal with. While he enjoys this contact with his assistants and his archivist, there is no doubt that the continuous concern of the day is his drawing.'

The office was closed, and there were fewer demands. He still had plenty to do, including work on *Mr Filkins in the Desert*, commissions for magazines, designs for charities, and video tutorials for the Instagram account Isolation Art School. But he had more time on his hands. There was always a pencil, ballpoint pen, crayon or pen at hand, and different kinds of paper, from small sketchbooks to huge sheets of 'proper Daler-Rowney A3 watercolour paper'. All he had to do was pick these up and draw.

One favourite tool is the chinagraph pencil. Made of hardened wax and developed for marking ceramics and other shiny surfaces like glass or acetate, it gives a soft, flexible line. A small gallery of thoughtful, inquiring china-graph men were drawn on low-quality brown paper, and more appeared in a delicately festive light blue, for no particular reason, on Christmas Day 2020.

Young Faces, 2019. Chinagraph pencil on watercolour paper

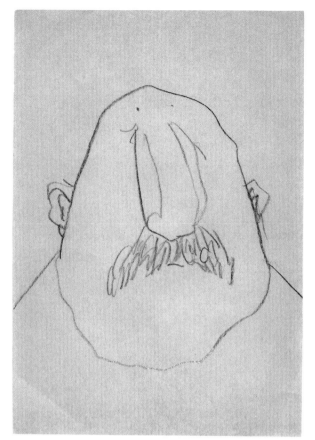

' I start with a forehead or a cheek or a nose, and
  perhaps there, there is enough for me to set off
  and discover the person as I draw them.' QB

Small Chinagraph Men, 2020. Chinagraph pencil on low-quality paper

Imaginary Portraits of Men, 2020. Light-blue chinagraph pencil on drawingbook paper

' When I do these I am not thinking of particular people, and
in fact, what is interesting to me is that I seem to discover
a character in drawing it. He or she comes into being on
the page. I never think of individual or particular people.
Incidentally, I can draw from life, although I very rarely do it.
Perhaps I should do more… I am very happy to have portraits
of my father and some of my friends from earlier life.' **QB**

Grey Faces, 2021. Oil pastel on cartridge paper

Sombre drawings, on grey paper, marked the start of the New Year – this time in oil pastel. But a new, more vibrant effect was produced when he used Sennelier oil pastels. These thick, waxy crayons were created by the manufacturer Henri Sennelier in Paris in 1949, for Picasso, who was hunting for something he could use on different surfaces without it cracking or fading; as soft as lipstick, they stay bright and can also be diluted to create a softer wash. In 2019 Quentin used black Sennelier pencils to create a large series of portraits, many of which were shown in exhibitions in London, at the Coningsby Gallery, and in Paris. But the pencils also come in a huge range of colours, and in a second Sennelier series, he turned to these. The mood alters in each one – formal, pensive, pugnacious, smiling, wistful, mischievous – imagined states of being, as well as imagined faces.

' Another interest for me is the structure of the head and the
way the medium – I have several to choose from – serves to
express it. It may be some economical open line technique,
which invites the spectator, with a little help, to imagine the
shape of the head; or it may be a question of accumulating
line as hatching or, with a softer medium, some kind of
shading to suggest the tone.' QB

Above and opposite: *Sennelier Portraits*, 2020. Oil pastel on drawing-book paper

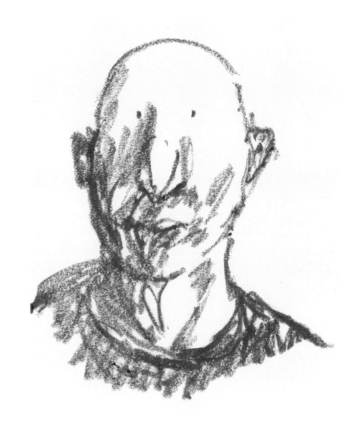

' I had the stub of a Sennelier oil stick in
  my studio in Hastings for a very long time.
  I had bought it on one of my regular trips
  to France, but just never used it. One day
  I picked it up and decided to see what it
  can do. I loved it, and that is how all this
  started… I find it fascinating to see all the
  different ways I can use just one oil stick
  to create so many different artistic effects.
  I keep trying to stop doing the portraits,
  but I can't – they just keep coming.' QB

The colourful sequence included both women and men. But Quentin finds that there is something different, if unquantifiable, about painting a woman's face: 'Perhaps they are more open, more ready to express emotions than men,' he wonders.

'There's more variety of character in women's faces; men's faces are more variations of the same formula, so I'm not looking for individuals so much with them. The portraits of women are often more elaborate and worked into with shading of an almost academic kind. And of course they have to have hair...' QB

Above and opposite: *Sennelier Portraits*, 2020. Oil pastel on drawing-book paper

Several of the coloured Sennelier portraits were sold at Hastings Contemporary. And as the series went on, the strokes became softer and the subtle effects of shading more pronounced, emphasizing the portrait's mood. Some of the Sennelier people, particularly those who have expressive single dots for eyes, seem to have no gender, or to share qualities of male and female. Gradually, these drawings tipped from realism into familiar, anxious grotesques, with sprouting eyes and thrusting mouth, reminding us of the stone heads, suggesting almost a reluctance to be there at all.

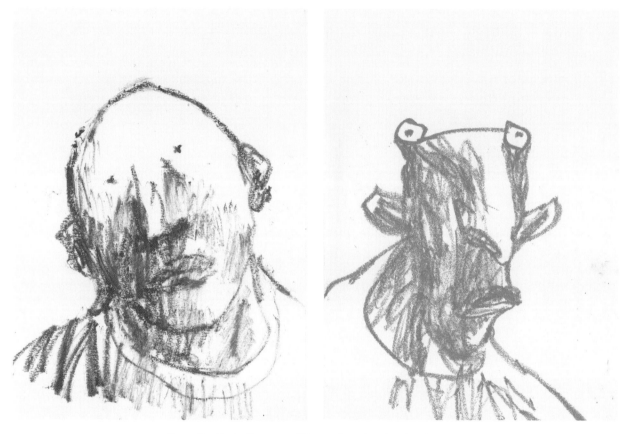

Sennelier Portraits, 2020. Oil pastel on drawing-book paper

The tenderness and compassionate fellow feeling in the Sennelier works are felt equally strongly in the sharper, clearer images that Quentin created with Stabilo pencils - coloured graphite pencils - in early 2021. They have a feeling of detached scrutiny - but whether the portrait is scrutinizing the artist or the other way round is a matter of doubt.

' I'm fascinated by portraits. One of the things about them
is that you get in touch with what people are thinking, or
possibly feeling, so that you take on that emotion, or that face,
and then of course that moves you on to the next… I don't
know what each one is to be, except if the last face was plump,
this one might be gaunt, or if the last one was innocent, then
the next might be complacent or supercilious.' **QB**

Stabilo Portraits, 2021. Stabilo pencil on drawing-book paper

The easy line of these pencils, so effective in outline and in the shading of the face, gives immediacy of expression. But it also asks for a kind of play-fulness – leaping lines, minimal detail. In another set of portraits, a single gesture tells all: a solid man, slightly grizzled or wrinkled, full of confidence, sitting back and touching his chin, perhaps about to ask a question; another, just as bulky, standing up, his hand raised to make a point. Perhaps they are having a discussion, or a business meeting, or talking about the best way to hook a salmon?

These drawings have an odd effect, making you look back and forth, first at the whole, the portrait of a person in the body, then at the faces – how can one convey so much by dot eyes, and a scribble?

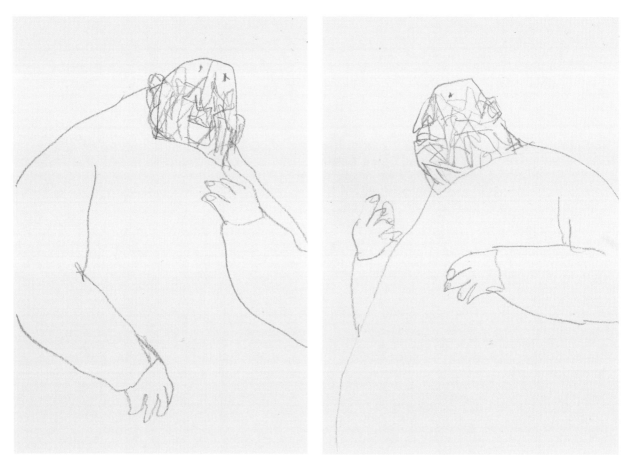

Men with Gesturing Arms, 2021. Stabilo pencil on drawing-book paper

Portraits in Watercolour Marker, 2021. Watercolour marker on drawing-book paper

If the men with gesturing arms use the drama of lines in an empty space, a different technique makes us feel bulk and solidity – no less mysterious for that. Every now and then Quentin uses watercolour markers, which give both an outline and, when you add water, a watercolour wash, which carries the colour and the tone of the portrait into another dimension. The effect can be quite solemn, and perhaps because the colours are so strong and artificial, they impart a particular mood, removing the imaginary portrait even further from 'real life' than a line drawing in pencil or pastel.

Whatever medium Quentin Blake uses, his 'Imaginary Portraits' feel 'real'. While the figures come from his imagination, or are discovered in the very process of drawing, we recognize all these men and women, even those with eyes on their heads. We can use our own imagination to make them breathe and think, and let us glimpse the possibility of their inner lives.

11

The Joy of Biro

The Unexpected Line

Quentin's imaginary portraits are drawn with crayon, oil pastels, pencil, ink, watercolour. But, he notes, 'The other implement which I find myself using more and more perhaps came as a bit of a surprise to me. It's what we call, in common language, a biro, although in fact most of the ones I use are not that, but in fact a ballpoint pen, of which I have several kinds.'

Ballpoint is a democratic medium, in reach of us all, and however sophisticated the technique, the way a biro sweeps on easily in the hand gives a kind of informal or primitive feel. No recognized artist appears to have taken ballpoint seriously before – but when Quentin picked up his biro he showed that its unvarying line could be adapted to all styles and moods: smooth, romantic, craggy or wild.

8 × 5 inch Biro Ladies, 2020
All illustrations in this chapter were drawn in ballpoint pen on drawing-book paper

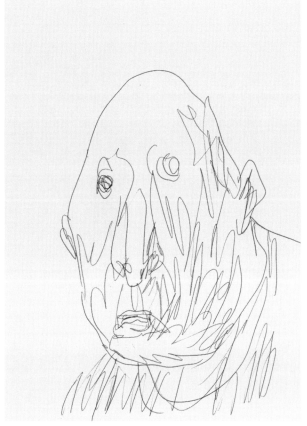

Topmost Male Biro Heads, 2021

Women's Heads (left) and *Men's and Women's Heads*, 2021

The portraits form part of a much larger collection, *Art of the Ballpoint*. Once he was hooked, Quentin's biro addiction took hold. In the summer and autumn of 2021 he began producing more and more sequences, with around twenty to thirty drawings in each series, some fantastic, some realistic, all full of verve. Some drawings are as small as 14 × 10 cm (5 × 4 inches), others are huge, 76 × 56 cm (30 × 22 inches). He could work with a single line, with squiggly detail or with complex shading. Ballpoint let him work at speed: some drawings that seem subtle and ripe with thought took only minutes. The profile of a girl, done in December 2020, immediately evokes a real person, appearing briefly in our lives as if she was just on her way somewhere, glimpsed for a moment basking in unexpected winter sun. By contrast, a month later, a Thurber-like sketch is a dry, ironic take on what one might call a 'dapper man'.

Above: *Men Quite Edwardian*, 2021
Opposite: *Biro Ladies*, 2020

However rapid the work, the sketches contain a lifetime of empathetic observation. Look, for example, at the paired studies of women's faces, or the bent-backed man leaning on his stick, feeling the ache of his curved spine, the tangled lines of his face conjuring a glance of bewilderment or suspicion. Or the woman bending forward, deep in concentration, drawn in a much denser style.

Faces of Two Women, 2020

' What is curious about a ballpoint pen as
  an art implement is that there is very little
  variation produced by pressure – it's a regular
  line all the time, but it's interesting to find ways
  of producing substance on the page.' **QB**

Leaning Woman, 2021

Gentlemen in Retirement, 2021

From the autumn of 2020 the sketches began to accumulate, and needed to be recorded and kept safe. Every afternoon his friend Linda Kitson came to his studio to talk over the work and photograph the drawings, recording the date, the size, the series. In her view, the biro heads may be the most striking set of drawings he has ever done: 'The funniest and the saddest, and the most skilful... Some with single open line, some with "crazy" shading in all directions, some with "classical" edge-to-edge shading. It's in the very minimal ones that you really need to know your anatomy, and in the fully worked ones that you need to know about volume.' All that knowledge is hidden beneath the easy-looking lines.

Many of the biro drawings fall into series, or 'families'. One acute, funny group is *Scientists Taking Notes*, a batch of boffins. Detail counts: somehow the coat collars and the pencils in their pockets identify them straight away. Apart from the exuberant arm-waving man who has, perhaps, stumbled upon a great discovery, all these long-coated men look disconcertingly self-important

Above and opposite: *Scientists Taking Notes*, 2020–1

and supercilious. This doesn't reflect a distrust of science on Quentin's part, rather a wariness of any group who see themselves as specialists, standing above the crowd.

Another series, equally evocative of theatre and mime, depicts chatelaines, massive women bearing comically small bunches of keys, like beings from some old French fairy tale.

Above and opposite: *Chatelaines*, 2021

' I don't know where the chatelaines came from, sometimes these people just turn up on the page... Incidentally, a part of the interest for me, apart from their individual characters, is the contrast between the large form, or whatever garment it is that they are wearing, and the small detail of their features and the little ring with the keys on it.' QB

Another set is labelled *Polish Aristocrats*. When asked about this title, Quentin's answer is simply, 'Well, that's who they are…'

Throughout the year Quentin's rolling ballpoint lines conjured different personalities and moods. Sometimes the drawings, like that of two men reading, where the easy style and composition seem to mirror their relaxed, engrossed mood, feel illustrative or naturalistic. Elsewhere, a moment or mood is defined by a gesture or stance that suggests something happening, that we can't quite see: a man leans back, the single lines outlining his body helping to emphasize the scribbled anxiety of his face and claw-like hands.

Polish Aristocrats, 2021

' I am not sure that the Polish aristocrats set out to be
that. They were figures of a certain elegance and poise
and I decided that must be what they are.' QB

Readers, Writers and Artists, 2021

Men with Worked Faces, 2021

As with the imaginary portraits, he homed in on the way that faces reveal different moods. In April 2021, defying the coming of spring, a group of *Miserable Men* emerged, some with long, looping lines looking like flop-eared basset hounds. Their cousins appeared the following month in a set of *Long Faces*, a double term of glumness and accurate description.

Any paper at hand could be used, even the squared paper of a small French exercise book, where the strong features of a middle-aged man push through the squares, demanding attention.

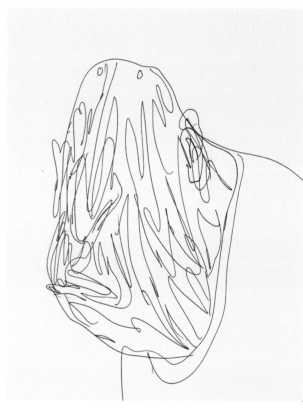

Man on Squared Paper, 2021

Miserable Men, 2021

Long Faces, 2021

Gradually, colour became more important. The red of the *Long Faces* that he drew in the heat of summer in July 2021 adds a formal, heraldic note. Conversely, the green of a boy's face, sketched in September, suggests innocence, like a growing thing; while the blue and red of a double face drawn in the same month feels like a flaring of mood, different personalities hiding behind a solemnly expressionless, near abstract mask. Where Quentin works his pen back and forth across the features in a version of cross-hatching, colour gives intensity of mood. The blue stands out first, giving the viewer a small shock before the lines of the face burn through.

In black-and-white ballpoint Quentin found he could gain a similarly intense effect, and feeling of solidity, through density of line. These large drawings feel deliberately 'scrambled', so that the features, at first, are obscured behind the net of lines, slowly gaining in clarity and power.

Boy, 2021   *Double Pen Portrait*, 2021

Woman's Face, Large, 2021   *Male Head in Coloured Ballpoint,* 2021

'One almost unique characteristic of a ballpoint pen is that it
scarcely at all responds to pressure (in that respect it's something
like engraving). You can only get shade by the accumulation of line.
Of course, you have to have in mind some idea of the structure
you're looking for, but in some drawings I have done what I think
of as conventional academic shading, and in others there is a sort
of anarchic cross-hatching. Then yet again there are possibilities in
just simply scribbling until you reach the tone you want.' QB

With great skill Quentin can also create ballpoint shading with the simplest up and down strokes, amplifying expressiveness in an almost traditional manner, as in his moving drawing of a troubled person made in August 2021. And in one huge 'heroic' drawing, where the close lines leave no space at all, the dense shading endows a near-classical head with a brooding dignity. As Linda Kitson says, 'a fully modelled head on this scale is an awesome thing.'

Quentin may be ferociously preoccupied by a theme, or, in this case, a particular drawing medium, but he's rarely stuck in a rut. At the same time as he was experimenting with academic shading in the anxious man and the dark face, he could produce a magically simple portrait, in a few confident lines – a girl, staring ahead, as if posing for a Renaissance bust.

' One aspect that appealed to me was the idea of a relatively large drawing that could only be created by the accumulation of small lines; and the idea that this small pedestrian implement could produce something on an imposing scale.' QB

Above: Quentin in the studio with *Heroic Head*, 2021
Opposite: *Heroic Head*, 2021

Girl, Profile, 2021

The line itself has life, as it does in a drawing by Matisse. There's a sense of spontaneity, as if the pen finds its own way, teasing the artist. Intrigued by new possibilities, Quentin approaches them with the poise of a dancer on a wire who makes something difficult look like a stroll in a field. In the autumn of 2021, intrigued to hear that the British Library was eager to make itself more 'family-friendly', he thought that a ballpoint exhibition might fit in well there. The very idea of such a show 'in some significant intellectual situation' immediately inspired another family-friendly sequence. In this he revived one of his liveliest themes, the circus, celebrated in his book *Angelo* and in the hospital murals *Our Friends in the Circus*. In his biro drawings dazzling feats are performed. The audience bend backwards, straining up to see an acrobat on the tightrope high above, smiling at the birds on his pole.

Opposite: *Anxious Face*, 2021

Small dogs gawp at a pig in the air, or look on doubtfully when invited to jump through a hoop - taking us back to all the birds and animals that have inhabited Quentin Blake's books, helping us to see what is going on.

The drawings are like Alexander Calder's mobiles, wires hanging from the ceiling, swaying in a breeze, catching shafts of light, delicate as silk in the pale biro colours. But in the ballpoint circus, amateurs can also have a go, clutching a glass and a sandwich, burying their nose in a newspaper, careless of gravity's pull. 'Ooops' is the only reaction. Quentin knows aiming high is difficult. But he tells us, too, that imagination can let us soar. If we tumble, for a moment we can at least know what it feels like to fly.

Above and opposite: *The Ballpoint Circus*, 2021

Thinking of ways that children and adults could all join in, he created another series, *One Line or Two*, where you try to trace the individual lines that make up the portraits. It's also an invitation to do your own drawings - keep that pen on the paper and the result may turn out to be surprisingly characterful and odd.

An exhibition of ballpoint drawings at the Hastings Contemporary in the spring of 2022 demonstrated how much 'enjoyment' is inherent in Quentin's practice. Part of his delight in biro is the idea that everyone can have a go and see what turns up. In Quentin's art - in his illustrations for other writers, his own books, his lonely travellers and his portraits - something is always happening, anarchic, unexpected, ridiculous, joyful, mischievous, poignant. He is an artist with a powerful, often strange imagination who wants to make direct, living, vital, fresh contact with the real world. And he always looks ahead. There's no conclusion to this book. As he moves into his nineties, all we can do is ask, 'What will Quentin Blake do next?'

Above and opposite: *One Line or Two?*, 2021

'I think it's quite hard to work out but it's very easy to do – and you can produce quite a complicated drawing with one line as long as you remember not to take the pen off the paper.' QB

Author's Note

Quotations from Quentin Blake are taken from various sources, including personal conversations and correspondence, as well as interviews, articles, videos, radio and television appearances – among them the BBC documentary *Quentin Blake: The Drawing of My Life*, screened in December 2021. Many of his comments about individual works can be found on his official website: www.quentinblake.com. Other quotations from Quentin can be found in Joanna Carey's *Quentin Blake* (Tate Publishing, 2014) and Ghislaine Kenyon's *Quentin Blake: In the Theatre of the Imagination* (Bloomsbury, 2016). But the most important sources are his own books: *Words and Pictures* (Jonathan Cape, 2000), *Beyond the Page* (Tate Publishing, 2012), *Pens, Ink & Places* (Tate Publishing, 2018) and *A Year of Drawings* (Thames & Hudson, 2021).

I have had a happy time working on this book, chiefly thanks to Quentin himself, an invigorating presence and inspiring artist. I am grateful to Claudia Zeff, Quentin's consultant and Deputy Chair of the House of Illustration, who has orchestrated this project with calm and charm. Linda Kitson made an invaluable contribution to the final chapters, while Quentin's assistants, Nikki Mansergh and Sarah Edwards, have been a fund of prompt and cheerful help. I owe particular thanks to the Quentin Blake archivist, Liz Williams, who has provided details of all images, exhibitions and publications, and never seemed fazed by odd requests and demands. Zoe Waldie at Rogers, Coleridge and White has, as always, been a great support, while many thanks must go to Roger Thorp and Mohara Gill at Thames & Hudson, to my editor, Emma Barton, and to the designer, Sarah Praill, and the whole production team, for making this book so beautiful and alive.

Off to something new

Select Bibliography

The below list collates all the works illustrated by Quentin Blake mentioned in this book. A full bibliography of all first-edition works illustrated by Blake can be found on his website: www.quentinblake.com.

Amis, Kingsley, *Lucky Jim* (Penguin, 1961)

Apuleius, *The Golden Ass*, trans. E. J. Kenney (The Folio Society, 2015)

Aristophanes, *The Birds*, trans. Dudley Fitts (Lion & Unicorn Press, 1971)

Beckett, Samuel, *Waiting for Godot* (The Folio Society, 2021)

Bergerac, Cyrano de, *Voyages to the Moon and the Sun*, trans. Richard Aldington (The Folio Society, 1991)

Blake, Quentin, *Patrick* (Jonathan Cape, 1968)

Blake, Quentin, *Jack and Nancy* (Jonathan Cape, 1969)

Blake, Quentin, *Angelo* (Jonathan Cape, 1970)

Blake, Quentin, *Mister Magnolia* (Jonathan Cape, 1980)

Blake, Quentin, *The Story of the Dancing Frog* (Jonathan Cape, 1984)

Blake, Quentin, *Mrs Armitage on Wheels* (Jonathan Cape, 1987)

Blake, Quentin, *All Join In* (Jonathan Cape, 1990)

Blake, Quentin, *Cockatoos* (Jonathan Cape, 1992)

Blake, Quentin, *Simpkin* (Jonathan Cape, 1993)

Blake, Quentin, *Clown* (Jonathan Cape, 1995)

Blake, Quentin, *The Green Ship* (Jonathan Cape, 1998)

Blake, Quentin, *Zagazoo* (Jonathan Cape, 1998)

Blake, Quentin, with Russell Hoban (intro.), *Woman with a Book* (Camberwell Press, 1999)

Blake, Quentin, *Un bateau dans le ciel* (Rue du Monde, 2000)

Blake, Quentin, *Loveykins* (Jonathan Cape, 2002)

Blake, Quentin, *Mrs Armitage, Queen of the Road* (Jonathan Cape, 2003)

Blake, Quentin, *Angel Pavement* (Jonathan Cape, 2004)

Blake, Quentin, with Peter Campbell (intro.), *The Life of Birds* (Doubleday, 2005)

Blake, Quentin, *Beyond the Page* (Tate Publishing, 2012)

Blake, Quentin (ed.), with Sarah Bakewell (intro.), *Fifty Fables of La Fontaine*, trans. Norman R. Shapiro (The Folio Society, 2013)

Blake, Quentin, *Pens, Ink and Places* (Tate Publishing, 2018)

Blake, Quentin, and Will Self, *Moonlight Travellers* (Thames & Hudson, 2019)

Blake, Quentin, *The QB Papers* (Quentin Blake, 2019–20)

Blake, Quentin, *The Weed* (Tate Publishing, 2020)

Blake, Quentin, *Mr Filkins in the Desert* (Tate Publishing, 2021)

Bradbury, Malcolm, *Eating People is Wrong* (Penguin, 1962)

Carroll, Lewis, *The Hunting of the Snark* (The Folio Society, 1976)

Cervantes, Miguel de, *Don Quixote de la Mancha* (The Folio Society, 1995)

Dahl, Roald, *The Enormous Crocodile* (Jonathan Cape, 1978)

Dahl, Roald, *The Twits* (Jonathan Cape, 1980)

Dahl, Roald, *George's Marvellous Medicine* (Jonathan Cape, 1981)

Dahl, Roald, *The BFG* (Jonathan Cape, 1982)

Dahl, Roald, *Roald Dahl's Revolting Rhymes* (Jonathan Cape, 1982)

Dahl, Roald, *The Witches* (Jonathan Cape, 1983)

Dahl, Roald, *The Giraffe and the Pelly and Me* (Jonathan Cape, 1985)

Dahl, Roald, *Matilda* (Jonathan Cape, 1988)

Dahl, Roald, *Esio Trot* (Jonathan Cape, 1990)

Dahl, Roald, *My Year* (Jonathan Cape, 1993)

Dahl, Roald, *Danny the Champion of the World* (Jonathan Cape, 1994)

Dahl, Roald, *Charlie and the Chocolate Factory* (Viking, 1995)

Dahl, Roald, *James and the Giant Peach* (Viking, 1995)

Dahl, Roald, *Fantastic Mr Fox* (Viking, 1996)

Dahl, Roald, *The Roald Dahl Treasury* (Jonathan Cape, 1997)

Dahl, Roald, *Boy* (Jonathan Cape, 2012)

Dahl, Roald, *Billy and the Minpins* (Penguin Random House, 2017)

Gibbons, Stella, *Cold Comfort Farm* (The Folio Society, 1977)

Hoban, Russell, *How Tom Beat Captain Najork and His Hired Sportsmen* (Jonathan Cape, 1974)

Hoban, Russell, *The Rain Door* (Gollancz, 1986)

Hoban, Russell, *Monsters* (Gollancz, 1989)

Hoban, Russell, *Trouble on Thunder Mountain* (Faber & Faber, 1999)

Hoban, Russell, *Rosie's Magic Horse* (Walker Books, 2012)

Hoban, Russell, *Riddley Walker* (The Folio Society, 2017)

Hugo, Victor, with Quentin Blake (intro.), *The Hunchback of Notre Dame*, trans. Walter J. Cobb (The Folio Society, 1998)

Martin, J.P., *Uncle* (Jonathan Cape, 1964)

Martin, J.P., *Uncle Cleans Up* (Jonathan Cape, 1965)

Morpurgo, Michael (ed.), *Muck and Magic* (Mammoth, 1995)

Morpurgo, Michael (ed.), *Because a Fire Was in My Head* (Faber & Faber, 2001)

Morpurgo, Michael, and Jane Feaver, *Cock Crow* (Egmont, 2005)

Morpurgo, Michael, *On Angel Wings* (Egmont, 2006)

Morpurgo, Michael, *Didn't We Have a Lovely Time!* (Walker Books, 2016)

Orwell, George, *Animal Farm* (The Folio Society, 1984)

Potter, Beatrix, *The Tale of Kitty-in-Boots* (Frederick Warne, 2016)

Rosen, Michael, *Mind Your Own Business* (Andre Deutsch, 1974)

Rosen, Michael, *Quick, Let's Get Out of Here!* (Andre Deutsch, 1983)

Rosen, Michael, *Michael Rosen's Sad Book* (Walker, 2004)

Rosen, Michael, *On the Move: Poems about Migration* (Walker, 2020)

Ruskin, John, *The King of the Golden River* (Thames & Hudson, 2019)

Dr Seuss, *Great Day for Up!* (Beginner Books, 1974)

Voltaire, with Julian Barnes (intro.), *Candide*, trans. Tobias Smollett (The Folio Society, 2011)

Walliams, David, *The Boy in the Dress* (HarperCollins Children's Books, 2008)

Walliams, David, *Mr Stink* (HarperCollins Children's Books, 2009)

Waugh, Evelyn, with William Deedes (intro.), *Black Mischief* (The Folio Society, 1980)

Waugh, Evelyn, with James Cameron (intro.), *Scoop* (The Folio Society, 1982)

Yeoman, John, *A Drink of Water and Other Stories* (Faber & Faber, 1960)

Yeoman, John, *The Boy Who Sprouted Antlers* (Faber & Faber, 1961)

Yeoman, John, *The World's Laziest Duck and Other Amazing Records* (Andersen Press, 1967)

Yeoman, John, *Sixes and Sevens* (Blackie, 1971)

Yeoman, John, *Mouse Trouble* (Hamish Hamilton, 1972)

Yeoman, John, *The Wild Washerwomen* (Hamish Hamilton, 1979)

Yeoman, John, *The Hermit and the Bear* (Andre Deutsch, 1984)

Yeoman, John, *The Do-It-Yourself House that Jack Built* (Hamish Hamilton, 1994)

Yeoman, John, *Up with Birds!* (Hamish Hamilton, 1998)

Zeff, Claudia (ed.), *A Year of Drawings* (Thames & Hudson, 2021)

Index

Page references in *italics* refer to
illustrations

20 Bald Men 172-3, *173*
40 Women for Downing 154, *154*, 211

Adegbite, Opefoluwa Sarah 159
Alexandra Avenue Health & Social
  Care Unit 143, *143*
All Join In 75, *75*
Amis, Kingsley 23
Angel Pavement 8, 63, *63*
Angelo 2-3, 65, *65*, 245
Angers University Hospital 145-6,
  145, *146*
Apprehensive Girls and Women 204,
  206
Apuleius, *The Golden Ass* 120, *120*
Aristophanes, *The Birds* 30, *30*, *31*
'Arrows of Love' (2018) 149, *150*
Art of the Ballpoint 224-49

Baker, Christine 82
The Ballpoint Circus 245-6, *246*, *247*
Barnes, Julian 117
Barrault, Jean-Louis 14
Beckett, Samuel, *Waiting for Godot*
  124, *124*
Benson, Patrick 104
Bergerac, Cyrano de, *Voyages to the
  Moon and the Sun* 113, 115-17, *115*, *116*
Beyond the Page 56, 146
The Birds 30, *30-1*
Bradbury, Malcolm 23
British Library 63, 245

Calder, Alexander 246
Calman, Mel 149
Carné, Marcel 14
Carroll, Lewis, *Hunting of the Snark* 111
Cervantes, Miguel de, *Don Quixote* 7,
  111-13, *112*, *113*
Chance Encounters 174, *174*
Characters in Search of a Story (2012)
  150, *151*, 156

Chatelaines 234-35, *234*, *235*
Chazal, Gilles 132
Chelsea School of Art 24-6
Children with Birds & Dogs 158-9, *158*
'Children with Birds & Dogs' (2019)
  exhibition 211
Children's Laureate 7, 129
Children's Library, Hastings 162
Clown 68, *68*, *69*
Cockatoos 79, *79-81*
Companions 150, *151*
Constant Readers 170-1, *170*
Cruikshank, George 16

Dahl, Felicity 95
Dahl, Roald 88-109, *100*
  The BFG 92-5, *93-4*, 104
  Billy and the Minpins 104, *106*
  Boy: Tales of Childhood 104, *107*, 108
  Charlie and the Chocolate Factory
    101, *103*
  Danny, the Champion of the World
    104, *104*
  The Enormous Crocodile 89, *90*
  Esio Trot 101, *101*
  Fantastic Mr Fox 104, *105*
  George's Marvellous Medicine 91, *92*
  The Giraffe and the Pelly and Me 88-9,
    98, *100*
  James and the Giant Peach 96, 101,
    102
  Matilda 95-6, *95*
  My Year 108, *108*, *109*
  Roald Dahl's Revolting Rhymes 98,
    98, *99*
  The Twits 89, 91, *91*, 96
  The Witches 96, *96*, *97*
Daumier, Honoré 16
Downing College, Cambridge 18, 154,
  154, 211
Doyle, Dicky 16, 126-7
The Dragon Centre, St George's
  Hospital 144, *145*
English Parade 18
Eroded Heads 208

Feet in the Water 171, 172, *172*
Folio Society 111, 121
Foundling Museum 159, 211
François, André 18
Frederick Warne 125
French Institute 162

Galerie Martine Gossieaux 149, 156
Gilmore, Liz 160
Gordon Mental Health Centre 138,
  140, *141*
The Green Ship 4, 71, *71*, *72*
Grey Faces 215, *215*

Hand in Hand 164, *164-5*
Hastings Contemporary (Jerwood
  Gallery) 220, 248
  'Life Under Water' (2015) 160-2
  'The Only Way to Travel' (2017)
    179-80, *180-5*
  The Taxi Driver 200-3, *201*, *202*
  'We Live in Worrying Times'
    (2020-1) 7, 164, *164-5*, 202-3, 208
  'The World of Hats' (2018) 162-4,
    163
Heroic Head 242, *242*, *243*
High Places 192, *192*, *193*
Hoban, Russell 43-9, 168
  *How Tom Beat Captain Najork and his
    Hired Sportsmen* 43-4, *43*, *44*
  Monsters 45, *46-7*
  The Rain Door 45, *45*
  Riddley Walker 110-11, 121-3, *121*, *122*,
    123
  Rosie's Magic Horse 48, *49*
  Trouble on Thunder Mountain 48, *48*
Hôpital Armand Trousseau 143
House of Illustration 7, 9, 128
  'Arrows of Love' (2018) 149, *150*
Hugo, Victor, *Hunchback of Notre
  Dame* 113, *114*

Imaginary Portraits of Men 214
Insects 159-60, *159*

Jack and Nancy 64, 65
Jerwood Gallery *see* Hastings
   Contemporary
Jonathan Cape 41, 89
Jones, Nicolette 91–2

Kay, Jackie 159
Kenyon, Ghislaine 131, 161
Kershaw Ward, St Charles Hospital
   137–8, *137*, *138*
Kitson, Linda 179, 232, 242

La Fontaine, Jean de, *Fifty Fables of la
   Fontaine* 119, *119*
The Language of the Fan 175, *175*
Le Charivari 16
Leavis, F.R. 18
The Life of Birds 30, 78, *79*
Life Under Water 138, 140, *141*
'Life Under Water' (2015) 160–2, *160*,
   161, *162*
Long Faces 238–40, *239*
Loveykins 1, 77, *77*

'Magic Pencil' (2002) 63
Marlborough Gallery 150–3, 156
Martin, J.P., *Uncle* 41, *42*, 89
Maschler, Tom 89
Matisse, Henri 245
Men with Gesturing Arms 222, *223*
Miserable Men 238, *238*
Mr Filkins in the Desert 86, *86*, *87*, 212
Mister Magnolia 7, 66, 67, *67*, 71
Mrs Armitage, Queen of the Road 7, 70,
   71
Mrs Armitage on Wheels 7, 70, 71
Moonlight Travellers 182, *182–5*, 197
Morpurgo, Michael: *Because a Fire was
   in My Head* 51, *51*
   Didn't We Have a Lovely Time! 51, *52*
   Muck and Magic 50
   On Angel Wings 53, *53*
Morris Dancers 161, *162*
Mouse on a Tricycle 175, *176*, 176

National Gallery 129–31, *130*
The Nightingale Project 137–42
Northwick Park Hospital 138, *139*
'Nos Compagnons' (2014) 149, 156

Old and Young 150, *152*
On the Beach 197, *199*
One Line or Two 248–9, *248*, *249*
The Only Way to Travel 180, *181*, 198,
   200

'The Only Way to Travel' (2017)
   exhibition 179–80, *180–3*, 197
Our Friends in the Circus 138, *139*, 245

Patrick 60–1, *62*, *63*, 89
Penguin books 23, *23*, 104
Pens, Ink & Places 111, 179
The Perplexed 204, *205*
Petit Palais, Paris 131, *131*, 132
Picasso, Pablo 200, 215
Polish Aristocrats 236, *236*
Portraits in Watercolour Marker 223,
   223
Potter, Beatrix, *The Tale of Kitty-in-
   Boots* 125, *125*
Puffin books 108
Punch 7, 14–18, *14–17*

QB Papers 170–8, 188
Quentin Blake: The Drawing of My Life
   9, 95
'Quentin Blake et les Demoiselles des
   Bords de Seine' (2005) 131, *131*, 132

Riders by Night 174, *174*
Robb, Brian 24
Robinson, Heath 179
Rose, Andrea 63
Rosen, Michael 55–6, 159
   Michael Rosen's Sad Book 56, *57*, *58–9*
   Mind Your Own Business 53, 56
   On The Move: Poems about Migration
      203–5, *203*, *204*
   Quick, Let's Get Out of Here 56
Rosie Birth Centre 146, *147*
Ruskin, John, *The King of the Golden
   River* 126–7, *126–7*

Scenes at Twilight 171, 188
Scientists Taking Notes 232–4, *232*, *233*
Searle, Ronald 16
Seen at Twilight 188, *188–91*, 192
Self, Will 182
Sennelier, Henri 215
Sennelier Portraits 215–20
Seuss, Dr, *Great Day for Up!* 67
Simpkin 74, *75*
Small Chinagraph Men 212–13, *213*
Smollett, Tobias 117
Something Wrong Somewhere 204, *208*
Spectator 18–23
Sporting Women 153, *153*
Stabilo Portraits 220–3, *221*
Stanley Building 132, *133*, *134–5*
Stone Heads 196, 208–9, *209*

The Story of the Dancing Frog 73, *73*
Sunshine Travellers 194, *194*, *195*
The Taxi Driver 200–3, *201*, *202*
Tell Me a Picture (2001) 129–31, *130*
Tenniel, John 16
*Thirteen Things You Cannot Really
   Manage Without* 171, *175*, 177
Thorp, Roger 126

Un bateau dans le ciel 82, *83*
Unfortunates 204, *207*
University of Cambridge 132–3, *136*, 154

Vehicles of the Mind 179, *179*
Vélos Tout Terrain 186–8, *186*, *187*
Vincent Square Eating Disorder
   Service 141, *142*
Voltaire, *Candide, ou l'Optimisme* 7,
   117, *117*, *118*

Walliams, David: *The Boy in the Dress*
   53, *54*
   Mr Stink 53, *55*
Wayward Locks 154–5, *155*
'We Live in Worrying Times' (2020–1)
   7, 164, *164–5*, 202–3, *208*
The Weed 84, 85, *85*
Whitlock Blundell, Joe 111
Wildlife Artists of the Year 178, *178*
Williams, Liz 41
Wilson, Michael 129
Woman with a Book 166–9, *168–9*
Women & Creatures 148, 156, *157*
Women with Birds 156, *156*
Words and Pictures 14
'The World of Hats' (2018) 162–4, *163*

A Year of Drawings 192–5, 211–12
Yeoman, John 33–41
   The Boy Who Sprouted Antlers 36, *36*
   *The Do-It-Yourself House that Jack
      Built* 38, *39*
   A Drink of Water 33, *34*
   The Hermit and the Bear 38, *40*
   Mouse Trouble 37, *37*
   Sixes and Sevens 35, *35*
   Up with Birds! 41, *41*
   The Wild Washerwomen 32–3, 38, *38*
   *The World's Laziest Duck and other
      Amazing Records* 34
Young Faces 210, *212*
You're Only Young Twice 137, *138*

Zagazoo 75–7, *76*
Zeff, Claudia 149, 211–12

Jenny Uglow is a prize-winning author and biographer. Previous publications include biographies of Thomas Bewick and Edward Lear, which won the National Arts Writers Award and the Hawthornden Prize respectively. Her study of Walter Crane was published by Thames & Hudson in *The Illustrators* series in 2019.

Front cover: Quentin Blake: self-portrait, 2021
Back cover: Quentin with his work, 2007
Half-title page: *Loveykins*, 2002
Title page: *Angelo*, 1970
Contents page: *The Green Ship*, 1998

First published in the United Kingdom in 2022 by
Thames & Hudson Ltd, 181A High Holborn, London WC1V 7QX

First published in the United States of America in 2022 by
Thames & Hudson Inc., 500 Fifth Avenue, New York, New York 10110

Reprinted 2023

The Quentin Blake Book © 2022 Thames & Hudson Ltd, London

Text © 2022 Jenny Uglow

Illustrations © 2022 Quentin Blake, except as follows:

a: above; b: below; l: left; r: right
Andersen Press: 34b, 35; Photo © Burgess Studio: 171; Photo © Christophe Fouin: 132;
Hamish Hamilton: 39b; Jonathan Cape: 42; Jonathan Cape, © Russell Hoban: 121;
Photo © Linda Kitson: 145, 242; Penguin: 23; © Punch Limited: 14, 15, 16, 17; Scholastic:
56; © The Spectator: 18, 19, 20, 21, 22; Thames & Hudson, 2017/Faber & Faber, 1960: 34al;
Photo © Tom Thistlethwaite: 201, 202; Photo © Michael Walter/Troika: 133

Designed by Sarah Praill

British Library Cataloguing-in-Publication Data
A catalogue record for this book is available from the British Library

Library of Congress Control Number 2022931897

ISBN   978-0-500-09435-8

Printed and bound in China by RR Donnelley

Be the first to know about our new releases,
exclusive content and author events by visiting
thamesandhudson.com
thamesandhudsonusa.com
thamesandhudson.com.au

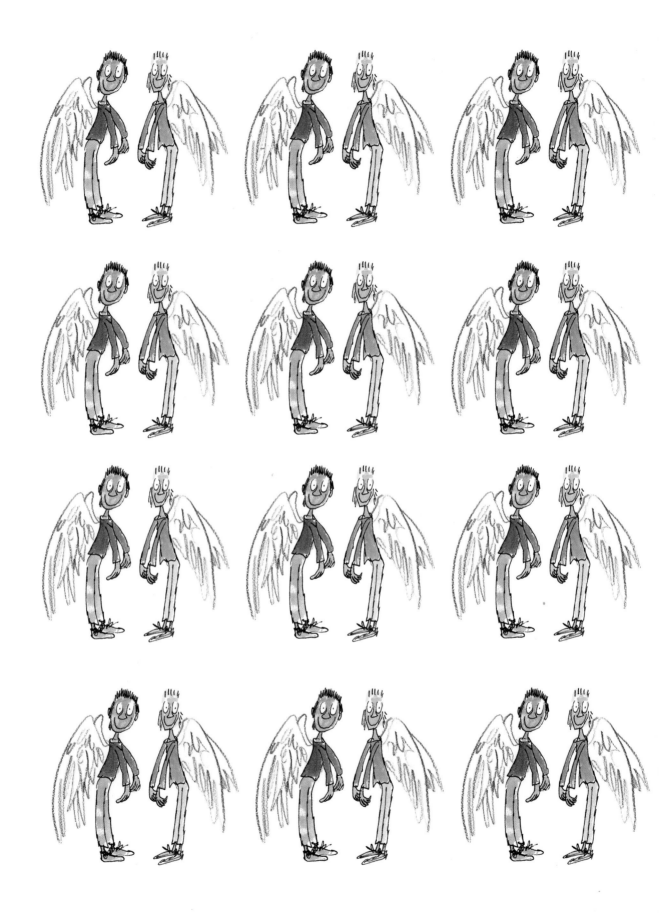